A How-to-Series Book

The Self-Publishing Encyclopedia

by

Gretchen & Al Beatty

Illustration & photography by the authors

GAB Publishing

Boise, Idaho

Published by
GAB Publishing
Boise, Idaho

ISBN 9781798115763

Distributed by
Kindle Direct Publishing an Amazon Company
http://www.amazon.com

BT's Fly Fishing Products
Boise, Idaho
http://www.btsflyfishing.com

Designed by Gretchen & Al Beatty
GAB Publishing, Boise, Idaho

DEDICATION

We dedicate this book to Gary LaFontaine, Chris Bessler, Dick Wentz, Judy Lehmberg, and Tracie Maler. All have helped shaped our journey into publishing's many forms including our newest venture, self-publishing. Without them it would have never been possible

ACKNOWLEDGEMENTS

We thank the many fly tiers we've known over the years who have willingly shared their knowledge with us. As a collective, they've provided inspiration and ideas that have spanned our complete publishing careers AND BEYOND thus allowing us to venture into this instructional volume, hopefully of value to ALL aspiring, self-publishing authors.

Amazon.com eBooks by the Beattys

How to WRITE A Fly Tying E-Book

How to Tie!! Wonder Wings

A Dozen Dubbing Techniques

Callibaetis Parachute

How to Tie!! Beginning Fly Tying

How to Tie!! LaFontaine's Legacy Flies

How to Tie!! Hair Wing Flies

How to Tie!! EZY Trout Flies

How to Make!! Never Fail Peanut Brittle

How to Make!! Never Fail Caramel & English Toffee

Print-Media Books by the Beattys

Beginning Fly Tying (POD)

Tying Hair Wing Flies (ORC)

Tying Hair Wing Flies (POD)

Fly Pattern Encyclopedia (FFF)

Rotary Fly-Tying Techniques (Amato)

Innovative Flies & Techniques (Amato)

LaFontaine's Legacy (Globe Pequot)

LaFontaine's Legacy (POD)

How to Tie!! Wonder Wings (POD)

A Dozen Dubbing Techniques (POD)

How to Tie!! EZY Trout Flies (POD)

The Self-Publishing Encyclopedia (POD)

How to WRITE A Fly Tying E-Book (POD)

Table of Contents

Why We Wrote This Book 6

Before Getting Started 7

Chapter 1—Looking Back 9

Chapter 2—Images & Illustrations 11

Chapter 3—The Cross Roads 17

Chapter 4—Electronic Media 25
- 4-A—MS Word Text—Setup 26
- 4-B—Table of Contents 30
- 4-C—Editing Pictures for Kindle 33
- 4-D—Text, Pictures, Copy Editing 36
- 4-E—The eBook Cover 42
- 4-F—Preparing for Publication 44
- 4-G—Publishing A Kindle eBook 46
- 4-H—Publishing A Downloadable PDF 50

Chapter 5—Print Media 53
- 5-A—Printing At Home 53
- 5-B—Print On Demand Publishing (POD) 57
- 5-C—The Manuscript Template 58
- 5-D—Editing Pictures For POD 60
- 5-E—Laying Out The Book 63
- 5-F—The Book's Cover 68
- 5-G—Copy & Format Editing 73
- 5-H—Publishing Your Manuscript 75
- 5-I —Multiple Publishing Platforms 81
- 5-J —Spines & Rebinding 82

Chapter 6—Audio and Video 85

Chapter 7—Closing Comments 101

About the Authors 103

Why We Wrote This Book

Inspirational ideas can materialize when you least expect them so we use the note app in our Smartphone to quickly capture them before our fading memory looses the concept, sometimes forever. Recently inspiration hit us while we were building a decorative rock barrier along one side of a back-yard, flower bed. Al was positioning and holding the rocks while Gretchen used a level and her towel to move dirt so the rock remained in the desired location.

The project was a perfect example of teamwork in action until Gretchen happened to comment she though we should write a "how-to" book on paperback publishing. She though it would be a good companion to the eBook we had recently uploaded to our Amazon.com books-for-sale library page.

The synergy of the concept soon had the ideas start pouring out of minds like water. Al grabbed his Smartphone and captured a number of notes for later use. Unfortunately the rock-wall project came to a screeching halt while we brainstormed how to structure the new book.

We recalled the frustration encounter trying to learn how to publish our first "illustration intensive" eBook while keeping the file sizes within the Kindle Direct Publishing (KDP) parameters. We wrongly assumed the eBook restrictions would be similar when we started our journey down the KDP paperback path. We were still self-publishing through Kindle so the requirements would be similar, right? Unfortunately , they were not!

They were similar to the skills we developed during a 25-year career in the print-media business (books and magazines) but the differences were substantial enough we had to completely redo our first paperback book TWICE! Why? We HAD to meet KDP's expectations while dealing with the limitations of our home-office computers. The new-to-us paperback process was one of the things we discussed there in the garden about the book Gretchen was proposing.

You know, we just couldn't leave the single book idea alone and as we got back to the rock project our conversation ran away with us. Before we knew it the proposed book had been brainstormed into a self-publishing encyclopedia covering everything from a home-owners association newsletter, electronic and paperback publishing, online video production, and anything else our inquisitive minds could dream up.

We decided to break the book into sections with each having its own subchapters. In so doing we could better take a subject like photography and review the demands each self-publishing discipline brought to the equation.

If you check the Table of Contents, you'll find that photography is in fact a very important aspect of any illustration-intensive self publishing project. Another important consideration is the text and how you format it. What works for an eBook doesn't even come close to the needs of a paperback publication.

Before letting your enthusiasm push you ahead in the book, **please review** the next section. Understanding its information is most important to comprehending what "*The Self-Publishing Encyclopedia*" has to offer. Check it out, it won't take long.

Before Getting Started

You should be reading this encyclopedia if you are pondering the question, "How in the heck do I progress from publishing a story or column in my club newsletter to sharing my message with a larger audience?" Of course, the words "club newsletter" in the last sentence could just as easily be changed to include home-owners news, online articles, written notes to friends, comments in a diary, or any message you'd like to record. That's the purpose of this book!

On the other hand, it does not teach you how to become an author; you'll have to develop those skills on your own. Instead, it will teach you how to access a much larger audience than you are currently reaching today. In fact, self-publishing via the Internet and Amazon reaches the entire WORLD! That thought is staggering and even though we've been writing books for a number of years, the size of the audience we've accessed via KPD is almost overwhelming!

We suspect you could be reading these words because you've found getting a print media publisher interested in your work to be a daunting task. Grabbing the attention of a **Self Publisher** is much easier. Why? It's because **YOU** are the publisher! Isn't that a crazy thought? You can become a published author and a successful publisher all at the same time. Now that really is mind-boggling!

Anyone who can shoot a picture and use text to explain what that picture represents CAN write a manuscript. Advancing from a single-page newsletter to a book's manuscript is what we'll be discussing in the next chapters.

If sharing your knowledge and skills is one of your goals then self publishing through KDP can be a positive addition to your educational bag-of-tricks. Besides, we found putting our skills, knowledge, and ideas into the written word pushed us to take a hard look at our instructions and fine tune them so they can be easily understood by a wide-ranging audience. So what does that mean? It means we (and that includes those of you reading these pages) must present our ideas and concepts with clearly written text that is not too difficult for younger students to understand. Like fly-tying and fishing legion Gary LaFontaine once told us, "Write so a sixth-grader can understand and ALL of your audience will get your point." In other words, keep your sentences simple so everyone from 8 to 88 gets your message.

The next few sentences hold the KEY to the whole book. It's IMPORTANT you read and understand them otherwise the information herein will make little sense.

We have used nothing but PCs since our first, 1985 dual-floppy IBM computer. Therefore all of our instructions are written focused on the **PC user** using the Control, Alt, and Shift keys. If you are a **MAC user**, you'll need to convert those keys to your system.

The text and layout programs we use throughout the book include **Word** and **Publisher** which are part of the **Microsoft Office 2007** lineup of software. Also, we organize and edit the photographs for our books using the **Window 7 Explorer** file-directory system and **Photoshop CS6** and **CC**. If you have different programs, you'll need to adjust accordingly. In these situations, we've found Google to be our friend. Last, we use the free **Grammarly** program to copy edit our text. It's not perfect but the subject matter we share is also not rocket science either. We'll discuss this subject in greater detail in a future chapter.

Chapter 1—Looking Back

Like many of you, over the years we've learned using the rear view mirror on our vehicle is a good way of keeping track of where we've been and what's coming up behind us. The fish-eye part of the mirror is especially helpful in identifying possible problems close on either side of the vehicle. Considering everything the rear view mirror brings to our driving safety there is still a blind spot on either side that requires us to carefully look on both sides of the vehicle before turning or making lane changes.

Our goal with this book is to explore the blind spots around our metaphorical vehicle in relation to today's connected world. From this point forward we'll be calling that vehicle, "self publishing as a form of communication."

Before we adventure into the new digital publishing world let's take a look back at just a few of the many self-publishing methods used through out man's history. Let's start with ancient men and women who captured their day-to-day lives via drawings on the cave walls of their homes. Are those drawings the first self-published "newsletters" of life at that point in history or are they just decorations to brighten a rather drab existence? We think they are a bit of both because they seem to depict people, animals, and activities typical of that point in time.

Fast forward several thousand years to the hieroglyphics as part of that period in history. They were the formal Ancient Egyptian writing system totaling about 1,000 distinct logographic, syllabic, and alphabetic elements. We think they definitely were a way of publishing information for that point in history. We assume professionals assembled the hieroglyphics but have seen pictures of crudes examples that appear to have been a form of self publishing. The key word in that last sentence is "assume" so don't take what we think as a statement of fact; reality could be something different.

As the years unfolded and we entered the time in history often referred to as "AD" indicated after the birth, life, and death of Jesus Christ the methods of self publishing change. We've read in our history books about town criers who's job was to share information not unlike a modern-day newsletter. The transmission method was audio rather than print but the information-sharing purpose was the same then as it is now.

This brings us to the point in history we'll call "recent past" where newspapers were the standard method for sharing information. During this period man advanced from riding a horse to town to learn the latest news and get the mail, to the typewriter, the mimeograph and Xerox machines, the computer, and the present-day cell phone.

During the more recent times in history the methods used to produce newspapers, books, and magazine have advanced from the world of the "paste up, black & white illustrations, and four-color separations" to the present day where anyone can become an author. What's even more incredible is YOU can also become a PUBLISHER with a little help from Amazon's Kindle Direct Publishing to take care of your printing and distribution needs.

What's even more unbelievable is you can do everything a publishing house used to do right in comfort of your home office. The only thing with which you need professional help is printing and binding your books if that is type of publishing you decide to use, however that is not the only option. If electronic publication is your choice then everything can easily be completed from your home office, lap-top computer, or even a cell phone. Electronic books (eBooks) are a fairly straight forward process. On the other hand the options available in the print and some electronic self-publishing areas are much broader. We'll explore them all as the next pages unfold.

We'll start our modern day self-publishing journey on the facing page with the image capturing process. Welcome to *The Self-Publishing Encyclopedia.*

Chapter 2—Images & Illustrations

At some point in history, a wise person once said, "A picture is worth a thousand words." The key words in that last sentence are "wise person." Whether it's worth a thousand words or not would have to be determined by the viewing audience and that could vary from one person to the next. We think the value of text versus picture is about a 60- to 40-percent mix. You'll have to decide which is 60 and which is 40 because few people learn the same way – one needs a picture and another needs text. EX: The two of us learn from different stimuli, (Al) needs to write or see information to retain it and (Gretchen) needs to see or hear the subject matter to place it in her mind's file cabinet.

No matter how you personally place information in your mind's file cabinet, it can't be overstated how much your student(s) will appreciate a well-shot picture as part of your instructional material. Guess what? A fly-tying book (print or electronic) is definitely a work of instructional material, and photography (and other imaging options) is our topic in this chapter.

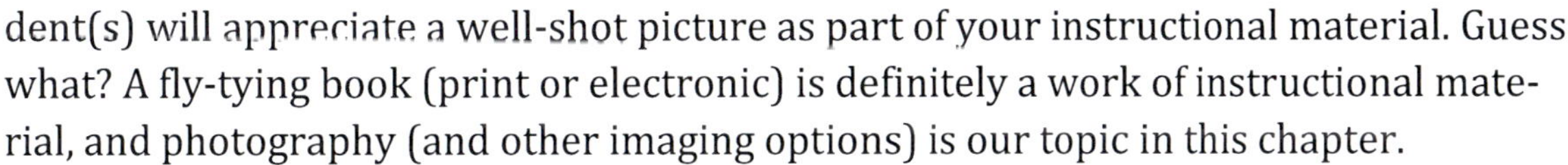

We're sorry but we have to talk about several boring topics before we get into the nuts and bolts of producing images for your Kindle Direct Publication (KDP) book. In the next few paragraphs, we'll briefly discuss the camera's sensor, resolution, and file formats you'll need for your KDP manuscript. If you are still using a film camera, now is the time to join the digital revolution or purchase a scanner to convert your film to digital. Therefore, we will not be discussing film processing (no Dektol or E-6 processing, thank you) or its use in digital publishing.

First let's discuss digital sensor size and yes, size does make a difference but not in the way you might suspect. Even though there are at least a dozen different sensor sizes in today's digital cameras, we'll focus on three because they are more popular. They are point and shoot (PS), crop sensor (CS), and full frame (FF).

Figure 2-1

Our photography setup is simple but flexible enough to meet our changing demands. We have several Manfrotto tripods and monopods. All of them have Quick Change Plates (QCP) so we can easily switch cameras around as needed. That includes several special clamps that allow us to mount our Smartphone(s) on a tripod if and when we wish. More on that in a few minutes.

We shoot photographs in any location the situation dictates but we do maintain a workstation in our office for most of our macro photography. That workstation (Figure 2-1) includes multiple backgrounds hung on a wall so we can quickly change them as needed. Standing in front of those backgrounds is a 4-wheel, movable table. Attached to the table is a specially-built, fly-tying vise that allows multiple angles to facilitate photographing the fly pattern from different points of view. This system easily produces step-by-step fly tying instructions but those of you focusing on other subjects may find a dedicated workstation less than helpful. An example would be a person writing a book on woodworking where a handheld camera would be the best option for illustrating how to make a cut on a table saw versus one on a sliding-arm, chop saw.

The last two items are a swing-arm lamp (to help see the subject while focusing) and several electronic flashes used to light the BACKGROUND ONLY. Most often we use the camera's onboard flash to light the subject (fly) but occasionally we add additional lighting based on the size of the subject (additional flashes or a ring light). That subject size could vary from a several-inch-long saltwater pattern, a complete box of flies, or any larger object.

Before continuing, let's discuss the background flashes. We keep several inexpensive **Yongnuo manual** flashes to use wherever more light is needed. It could be to lighten a background in a fly-pattern picture; to add detail in a dark room corner when doing real estate photography; or to use as a hair light when capturing a portrait. They only cost about $50.00 each on Amazon or eBay. The 460-II model we use has only three settings—M (manual), S1 (slave 1), and S2 (slave 2). We use the M & S1 modes when taking a picture using ALL manual settings on the camera and the flashes. When shooting fly-tying pictures, we usually use the A (aperture) setting with iTTL flash on our Nikon cameras (eTTL for you Canon shooters) to make the capture. TIP: If you are using the "A" setting (or any other semi-automatic exposure mode) on your camera BE SURE to adjust the external background flashes to the S2 setting. If you don't the camera's pre-flash will trip the external flashes too soon and they will have little if any effect on the picture. How do you think we figured that out? The hard way, of course!

The rolling table allows us to move it along with the vise & subject closer or further from the background to ensure we don't have unwanted shadows in the picture. Those pesky shadows can be very distracting so we make sure they don't appear in the photograph. On the facing page is a picture of our simple workstation to include background colors (with blue showing), two background flashes, and a homemade, multi-angle vise.

Figure 2-2

Our numerous Manfrotto tripods (and monopods) have served us well for many years. We're not trying to suggest you buy the same brand we have but really do recommend getting a tripod that includes some type of QCP. We do recommend you seriously consider purchasing a macro-focusing rail like the one to the right of the Smartphone in Figure 2-2. The macro focusing rail allows for back-and-forth or side-to-side adjustments. It is really helpful in lining up the subject (fly) so the picture isn't lopsided.

Any camera with a tripod hole will readily accept a QCP including a Smartphone with an attached tripod clamp. In Figure 2-2 above are (top left to right) Nikon Coolpix 995 with QCP, a Smartphone with a clamp and QCP, tripod-mounted macro-focusing rail, and (below) a Nikon DSLR with QCP.

TIP: A tripod and macro-focusing rail are not must-have pieces of equipment but they make it much easier to focus tight-macro shots. You can purchase one on eBay for about $50.00 (give to take). You'll have to decide if it's worth the cost.

Our cameras are many and range in type from a Smartphone to several high-end Nikons. They all do an excellent job and we wouldn't get rid of any of them. Setting that thought aside though, anyone with a Smartphone (who knows how to use it) can produce really good photographs for electronic media and when used for print media as long as the picture size doesn't exceed a half-page in width. Also, the darned things take great video footage; so good we use one for much of the content on our YouTube channel but that's a subject we'll review later in this book.

Our purpose here is to give you an idea of what your Smartphone can do for you and your instructional book. We think it is really helpful to set up a couple of items on your Smartphone camera. They are the on-camera flash and the voice activation command for taking pictures. The voice and/or timer release commands are especially helpful when the shot requires you to have one or both hands in the picture. We find the automatic setting on our Smartphone's camera exposure and focus to work just fine for our purposes.

For now, let's look at three pictures. Figure 2-3 is the Smartphone ready to take the photograph. Prior to taking this picture, Al used his fingers to "zoom" in on the fly so he could produce a tight (close) shot of it.

Figure 2-3

Figure 2-4 below was taken with ONLY the overhead, swing-arm lamp, no flash on the subject or the background, but there is some bounced light on the underside of the fly from the tinfoil reflector on the table. The picture is barely OK and not even close to great. Please notice there are no shadows on the background because all of the light is coming from the overhead lamp.

Figure 2-4

The first photograph on the facing page (Figure 2-5) was shot using the Smartphone's built-in flash to illuminate the fly but we DID NOT illuminate the background. Notice the shadow under the fly. It 's a better picture but the shadow is a little distracting. We could roll the table back far enough from the background to eliminate the shadow OR we could change the

Figure 2-5

angle of the flash by switching to a camera with the flash positioned slightly above the lens rather than directly adjacent like it is on the Smartphone.

Figure 2-6

We'll do so by removing the Smartphone from the tripod and replacing it with the Nikon Coolpix 995 as illustrated in Figure 2-6. We set the focus and exposure on the camera to automatic.

Figure 2-7

The first shot (Figure 2-7) with the 995 is with the onboard flash only, no extra light on the background.

Figure 2-8

Now let's take a look at the same shot after we turn on the two electronic flashes and illuminate the background. NOTE: We can easily change the shade of the blue background by increasing or decreasing the amount of light the two flashes put out. They are adjusted to a medium setting and set to the slave mode S2 so they fire at the same time as the flash on the camera.

Figure 2-9

Now we are dragging out the "big guns," the Nikon D750 with a 90-millimeter macro lens. In this photo (Figure 2-9) we have connected a USB cable between the camera and Al's computer. This connection allows him to adjust exposure and focus using the much larger computer screen. After all of the camera adjustments are set he takes the shot with a single click of the mouse.

Figure 2-10

This photo is as good as we are able to accomplish given our limited skill set. Compare Figure 2-10 with Figure 2-8 and see if you can find an almost $2,000.00 difference in camera/lens costs between the two. That's why we bring the Nikon Coolpix 995 to your attention. It's an incredible camera for eBook, website and smaller-size print-media pictures. Best of all you can purchase it on eBay (used-in-excellent-condition, 2019 prices) for about $50.00. Also, a Smartphone with its flash activated is another good choice. If this is your option, you'll have to move the background further away from the camera and use additional lighting to eliminate unwanted shadows behind or under the fly. We hope you'll agree and not use camera quality as an excuse to delay your venture into self-publishing.

We save ALL of our original from-the-camera pictures in a directory named after the book plus the designation OOC (out of camera). In the case of this book the directory is "EncyclopediaPics-OOC and inside that directory is another directory for edited pictures named "EncyclopediaPOD" that we'll actually "insert" into the book.

Chapter 3—The Cross Roads

We have only just started our self-publishing journey and we are already at an important intersection in a series of roads. Each road leads in a different direction AND the road we just traveled to reach this intersection is also very important. You might be wondering why in the heck we have a picture of our Dodge Ram and our Keystone Cougar 5th wheel (named the Cougar Cabin) placed here.

We assume if you are reading this book, you are interested in learning about self-publishing and you have also figured out our main interest is focused on the fly-fishing world. Yes, we use the below "Cabin" to travel to locations around our country in search of the next great adventure and story to go with it. We produced the draft outline for this book sitting beside, close to, or inside the "Cabin."

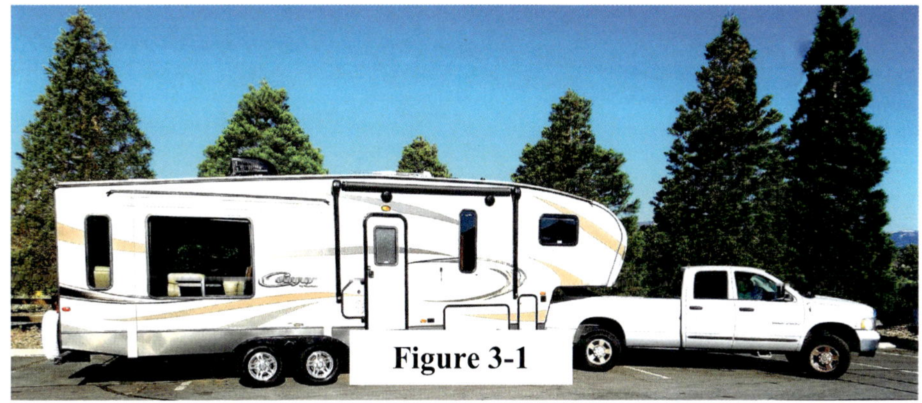

Figure 3-1

Setting aside the fact we travel and write; the picture above is an indicator we are at a crossroad in our self-publishing journey. Even though the old Dodge and the Cabin are sitting in a parking lot next to an outdoor store (Cabela's) in Reno, Nevada imagine for a minute it is actually sitting at a stop sign with three options regarding the direction we can choose to travel. Left takes us toward electronic self-publishing; straight ahead is on-the-paper print media; and to the right is video and audio production.

Each are topics we'll discuss in detail in future chapters. You may be wondering what we'll be discussing in this chapter when we've already identified the content for the rest of the book. Remember we are sitting at the imaginary stop sign and we had to travel a fourth road to reach it. It is the imaginary road we just traversed in Chapter 2 where we discussed capturing images. In this chapter, we'll briefly discuss a couple of other options for capturing images. The most important topic we'll explore here is what to do with those pictures once you capture them.

Remember back in Chapter 2 we discussed the importance of capturing the highest resolution image your equipment can produce? Let's take that thought further and state, "We suggest always using a camera with a minimum of a 12-megapixel sensor. If you can afford it a 16, 24 or more megapixel sensor is even better. It's easy to "throw away" some of the captured pixels if you don't need them but it's darned near impossible to add pixels you never captured in the first place. Yes, we already discussed this information but it's so important that we wanted to make sure you didn't miss it.

With that thought fresh in our mind's eye, let's establish a place to download and store those original, full-resolution pictures straight from the camera. We already have a **book directory** with two files in it. The first is the outline we wrote giving us a road map of our self-publishing journey. The second is the actual book pages we assembled in MS Publisher—the very pages you are now reading. We assume you all know how to make a new folder using Window Explorer (version 7 in our illustration). After building this most important folder for the original pictures the main book's directory should look like the one below in Figure 3-2 (sorry about the spelling error):

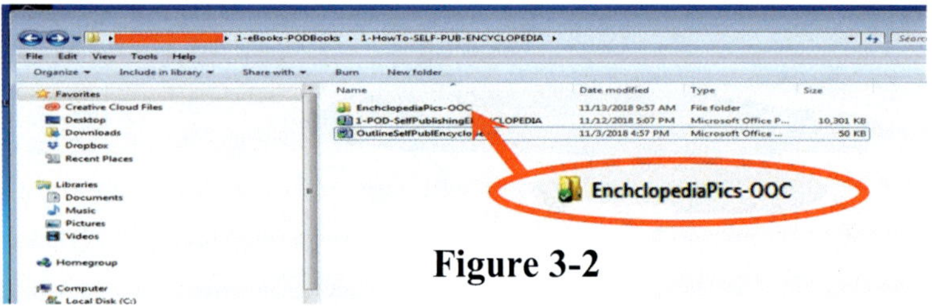

Figure 3-2

Notice the folder's title ends with the "OOC" designation. We use this to indicate the files within are the original out of camera files. We know we must NEVER change those files and always maintain the integrity of the original picture. It's really easy to leave the original file untouched by simply changing its name any time we make edits of any type. For this book when we edited the pictures you see throughout its pages, we added the 3-character "POD" suffix to each file. That suffix tells us the files are edited for a print-on-demand book and are stored in a folder SEPARATE, but inside, the OOC folder.

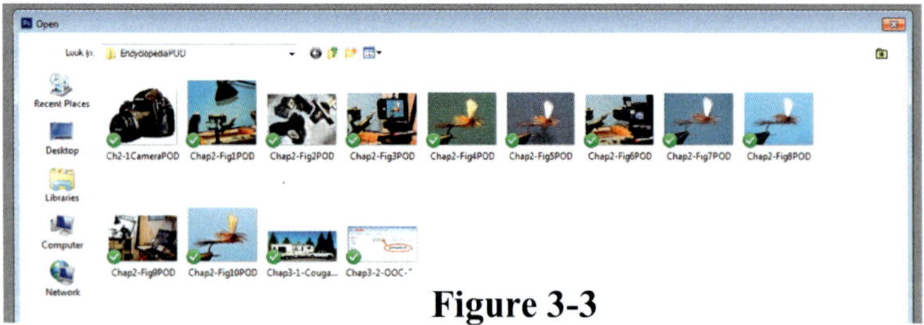

Figure 3-3

Figure 3-3 illustrates the POD folder with the picture files in place for this book up to this point in its progress. You can readily see that Figure 3-2 is the last picture we edited for this section EXCEPT for Figure 3-3 on which we were still working while writing this page.

Up to this point we hope you understand the importance of never "editing over" an original picture file AND that we think it's critical to save the edited picture in a folder just for a particular publishing discipline. In the case of this book (*The Self-Publishing Encyclopedia*), those files are saved into a folder called POD which is our designation for a print-on-demand paperback book.

Other Capture Options

Earlier in this chapter, we promised to share a couple of other ways of capturing images for use in any type of media discussed in this book. Our number one choice is usually a good quality digital camera but it's not always the answer. The previous page has two examples of images we used for this book that were not produced with a digital camera. Figures 2 & 3 are referred to as "**screen captures.**" That means they are a picture of what we saw on the screen at any given time. So, how do you capture the information on your computer screen and change it into a photograph?

There several ways to execute a screen capture including programs specifically for that purpose but we think our method is about as easy as pressing a single button. What button are we referencing? It the "PRT SC/SYS RQ button located on the top row of our computer next to the **F-12** and above the **ins** key. It is the "print screen" button and we'll refer to it as such from this point forward. In Figure 3-4, Al is pointing at the print screen button with a ballpoint pen.

Figure 3-4

So how do we use this button to capture a picture? First, understand a screen capture **does not** have the same high-quality resolution we can expect from any digital camera. Stated another way, we get better resolution from our old 3.2-megapixel Nikon 995 than we can expect from a screen capture. Knowing that bit of information means we must prepare our computer screen so only the information we want to capture is visible. Why? Because we do not want to crop the picture any more than needed. Note: In case you were not aware, **cropping** a picture **reduces resolution**. So we use the zoom feature in our various programs to make that part of the screen larger. In Photoshop that feature is set up under **Edit > Preferences > General >** then **click** the "Zoom with Scroll Wheel" **box**. Once that box is selected, just rotate the scroll wheel on the mouse to zoom in or out. When using the Microsoft Office Professional 2007 group of programs, the zooming in and out feature is a menu-selection option or it can be accomplish by holding down the Control key then rotating the scroll wheel on the mouse. We prefer using that method.

Right now you are probably thinking, “That sure is easy! I’ll just press the print screen button.” So, you press the button and nothing happens. Where is the screen capture? What the heck is going on? The reason you can’t see your screen capture is that it is hidden in the computer’s memory. We need to move the picture out of memory and into the real world using Photoshop.

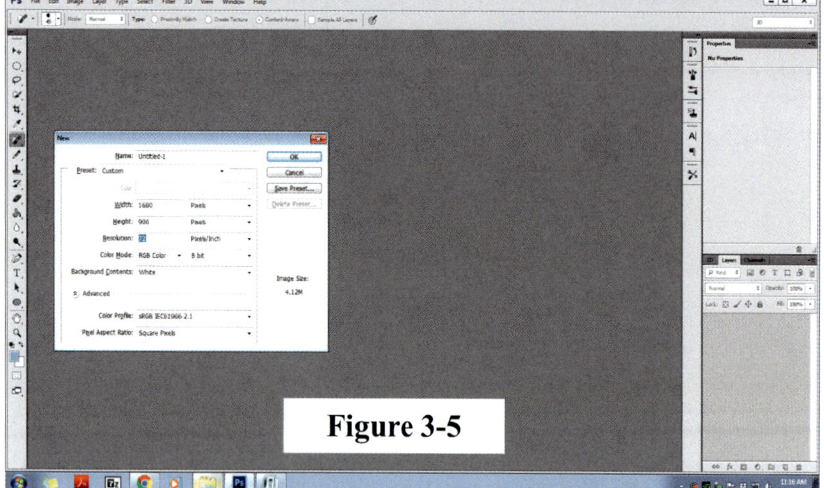
Figure 3-5

Let’s open Photoshop, then click **File > New** followed by pressing the enter button. Figure 3-5 is a screen capture of that Photoshop page with the “New” white, picture-option menu located at the center, left. You’ll probably notice it is difficult to clearly see the picture options available. That’s because we didn’t zoom in before we pressed the print screen button. Let’s zoom in on the “New” options box and press the print screen button again.

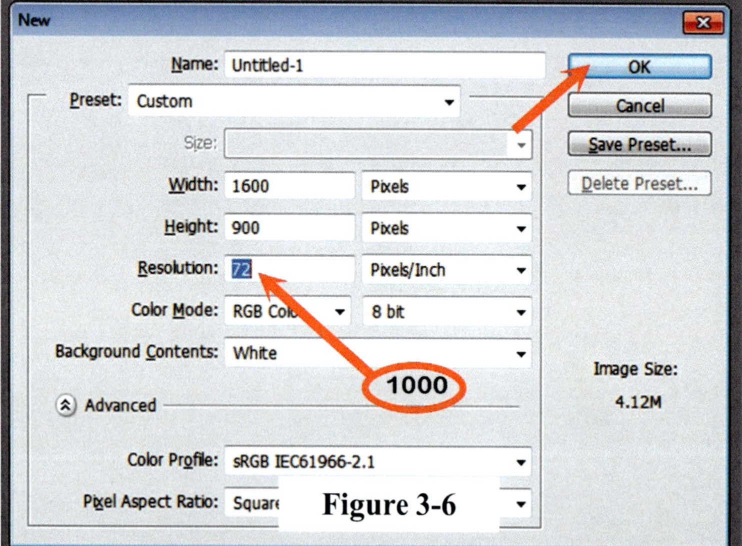

Figure 3-6

In Figure 3-6 it’s easier to see what’s happening in the options box. Notice we place the number “1000” in the lower center of the illustration, placed a red circle around it, and positioned an arrow pointing at the Resolution located under the Width and Height boxes. The default setting

Figure 3-7

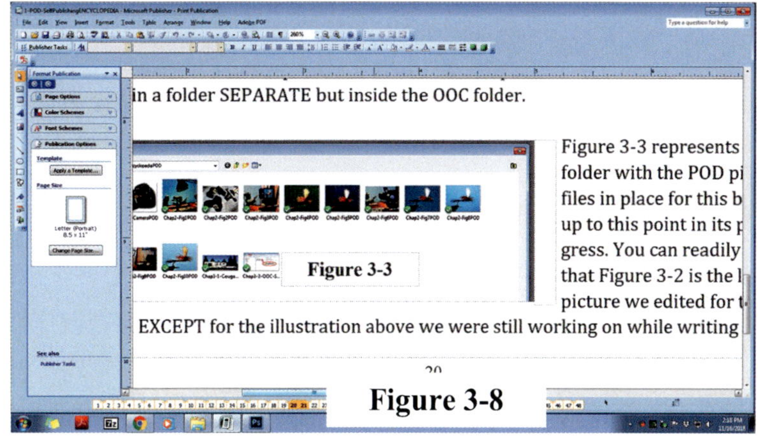

Figure 3-8

for the Resolution is 72 Pixel/Inch. After a lot of trial and error, we learned replacing the number "72" with "1000" produces a better looking screen capture. This change will keep the lines and numbers from having jagged edges in the final picture. Now press OK (top red arrow).

After clicking the OK button, Figure 3-7 is the next screen you can expect to see. While you were not looking we pressed the print screen button on a zoomed-in section of page 18` of this book. Doing so **copied** the expanded part of the page to the computer's memory. Once it was committed to memory we opened Photoshop with the blank picture frame illustrated in Figure 3-7 and pressed the Control + V keys to **paste** the screen capture into the blank picture frame. From this point we just edit, save, and use the screen capture (Figure 3-8) like we would any picture. Note: All of the Other Capture Options illustrations (except the picture of the computer keyboard) were screen captures made using the system we just outlined in the last several paragraphs. Are there other ways to do a screen capture? Of course there are but for us if the system is working, then we see no reason to change.

RAW, TIFF, and JPEG

We feel it's important to discuss this often controversial topic. It's possible for digital cameras (including cell phones) to capture images in RAW, TIFF or JPEG files. Scanners can capture images in TIFF, JPEG, and other non-picture formats based on the processing software used.

RAW images are a binary dump of data collected directly from a digital sensor. Unlike JPEG or TIFF files that can be easily opened, viewed and printed by almost all editing programs; RAW is a proprietary camera format and is not supported by all software programs. It has a LOT of editing latitude only stifled by the skills of the person editing the picture.

On the other hand, JPEG (jpg) or TIFF (tif) is an image the camera/scanner has applied automatic edits to the captured file based on settings that you enter into your camera or scanner via its menu system. Jpg and tif have LESS editing latitude but are much easier for a less experienced person to edit. Tif files (used for graphics publishing or medical imaging) are so large they soon slow our computers to a crawl.

Which format to use is up to you, the author, photographer, and editor. We use jpg files for almost all of our publishing needs but remember our advice earlier in this book? We suggested that YOU capture the highest quality image your camera can produce and do so on a regular basis. How! Almost all of our cameras except the old Nikon 995 have the ability to capture a RAW file AND a JPEG file at the same time and that's what we do via the camera's menu system (Figure 3-9).

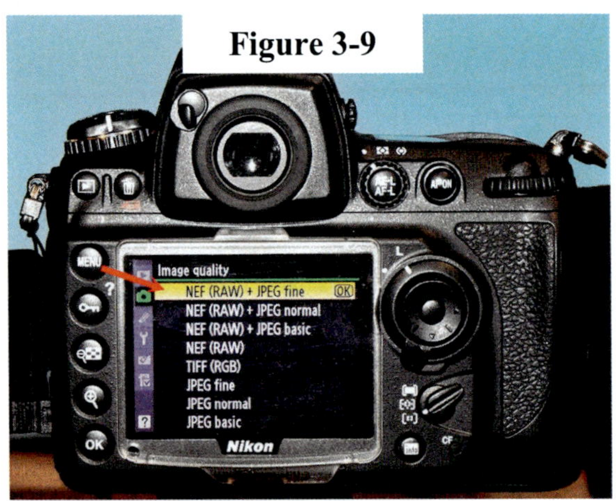

We save newly-captured RAW files in their own directory for use at some point in the future, then use the shot-at-the-same-time jpg file for our day-to-day work. The downside of this method is the RAW + Jpeg file option takes more memory (camera and computer). However, it gives us the opportunity to further edit the capture at some future date when technology may present us with a whole new range of options if we captured the information at the time we pressed the camera's shutter button rather than taking a jpg-only picture. In other words, save for the future (RAW) then use what's needed today (JPEG) based on current-day technology. At some point in a yet-to-come time, both of us will be glad we did! Think about it. In today's world, hard-drive and cloud-storage space is inexpensive.

The Scanner

Scanners are almost as useful as digital camera's when it comes to capturing pictures and illustrations. A scanner can capture much of what a digital camera can and it also is a better option for working with text conversion if that should be your objective. What do we mean by "text conversion?" It's a process by which we can scan a page of text then convert the scanned data into text using OCR (Optical Character Recognition) software.

That text can then be edited with MS Word or other similar program but it's not a process we'll review in this book. If you want to scan pages of text and convert them to files you can edit, it's something you'll need to learn separately from this document. Our purpose here is to use a scanner to produce illustrations for a self-published book. Quite frankly almost all people have a digital camera or a cell phone so using a scanner is what we'd call "old school" but there are still many of them in use today.

In the next few paragraphs, we'll share two methods for capturing images using the scanner. Let's start by capturing a digital image from a regular photograph of our daughter-in-law and grand daughter branding calves on the ranch. Notice in Figure 3-10, Al is holding the picture in front of the scanner and in Figure 3-11 is placing it on the flatbed face down. Figure 3-12 is a screen capture of the options he selected to scan the picture. You can get an idea of the items he used in the process by following the red arrows starting on the upper right side of the picture and traveling through the multiple screens he used to produce Figure 3-13.

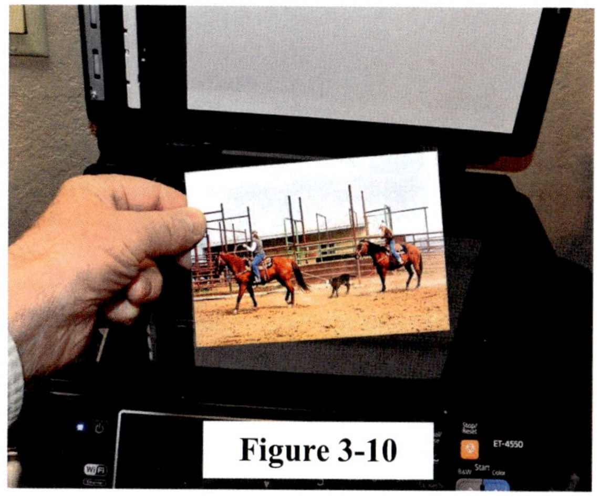

Figure 3-10

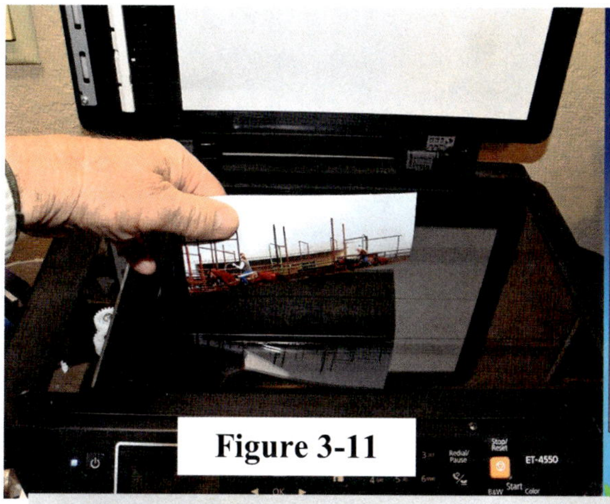

Figure 3-11

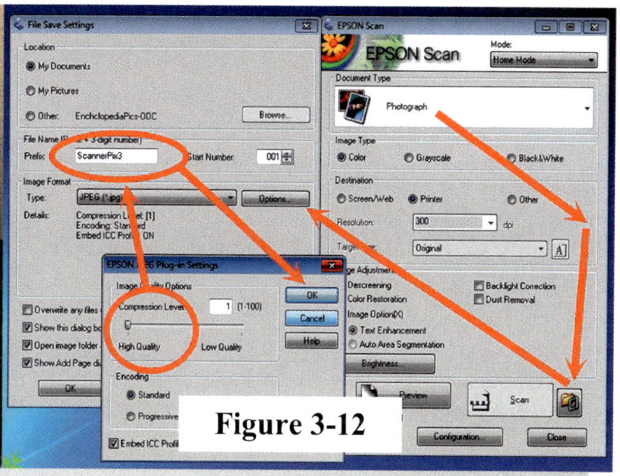

Figure 3-12

Figure 3-13

The photographs on this page illustrate that a scanner is a great option for capturing images of a printed picture, line drawing or any other object on flat material like a piece of paper. What do you think would happen if we place objects on the bed of the

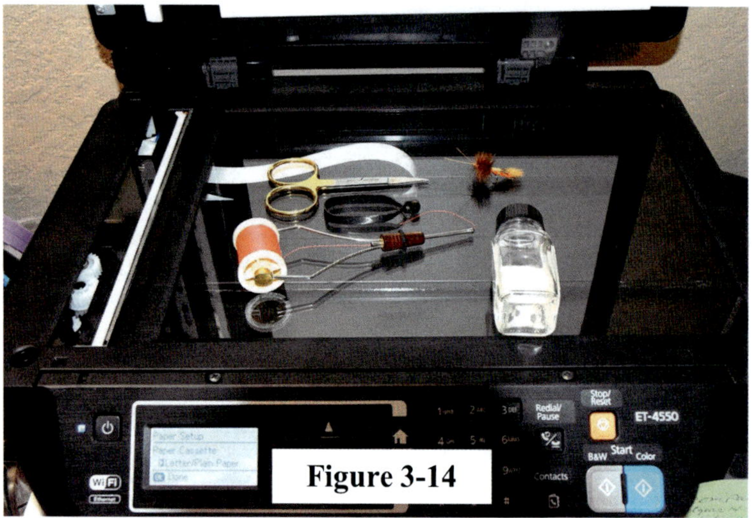

Figure 3-14

scanner that has dimension? As you'll soon see the scanner does a great job capturing items that are fairly flat but items with a lot of dimension are only in focus on the part of the image that actually is touching the bed of the scanner. Let's place several items from our fly-tying workbench on the scanner and show you what we mean. In Figure 3-14 you can see those items on the scanner's bed.

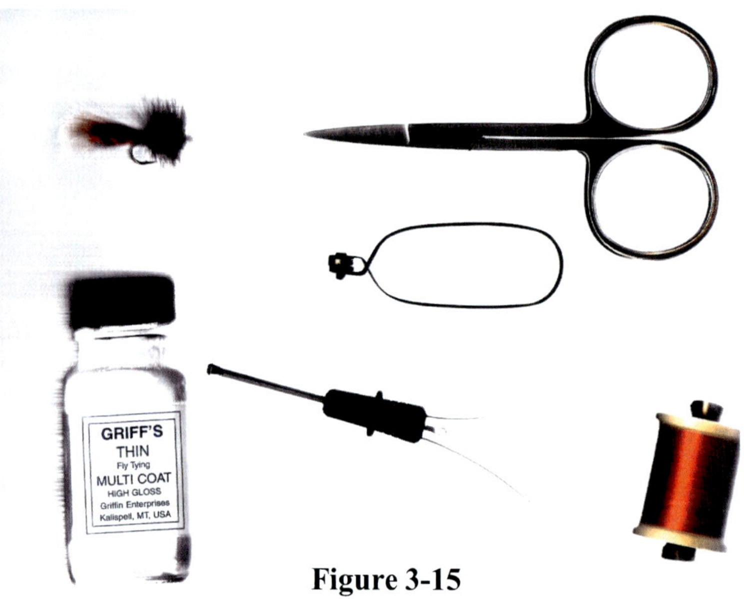

Figure 3-15

Figure 3-15 is the picture taken with the scanner after cropping it in Photoshop. The items in the picture are (top left to right) a fishing fly, scissors, hackle-feather pliers, bottle of head cement, and a bobbin with a spool of thread mounted in it. The scissors, pliers, and cement all look reasonably good in the photo. The other two items have too much dimension to render a decent picture because only a small portion of the object is in focus. Given the results in this picture, we think a scanner should not be your first self-publishing choice.

In some instances, tables, graphs, and charts can be taken directly from a program and converted to a JPG picture format. In the cases where the picture is a black and white image, we like to boost the contrast of the image in Photoshop to produce an illustration with more definition. Some people prefer saving this type of black and white image in a GIF file format but we really prefer the JPG formats. In so doing our files display the same in a Windows Explorer directory. Besides, Kindle will automatically convert any eBook picture you upload to JPG no matter which format is selected. Print books are converted to a PDF file before uploading so the format is less important.

Chapter 4—Electronic Media

It's taken us two whole chapters to get to the point where we are now at the same crossroads stop sign we were at the start of Chapter 2 with one major difference. We have a partially-full box (Windows Explorer directory) of original out-of-the-camera (OOC) pictures waiting to be used based on the direction we take from here. We also have a place (directory) to store additional pictures as we travel these pages.

Let's start the next step in our self-publishing journey by making a left turn and exploring our options with electronic publishing. The key word in that last sentence is "options." Your self-publishing options are almost mind-boggling. If you don't think they are then do a standard Google search using the words "self-publishing options." The search results are more pages of information than many of you (including us) have time to navigate. Almost all of those pages are companies wanting you to use THEIR service to self publish your work. How do we know? We spent almost all of three days following the search engine leads to their ultimate destination. ALL of them eventually led us to a page where we were supposed to give the company dollars in return for them "helping us" publish our work.

After a lot of searching and reading, we ended here with this book. Even though we call it an "encyclopedia" the book is really a detailed review of OUR journey only. That journey has been ALL with Amazon's Kindle Direct Publishing (KDP).

After many Google searches and a lot of reading, we finally determined KPD was the best option for us. As you read through these pages, you'll find we use that company for about 95 percent of our publishing needs. The other 5 percent will become obvious as we progress. We'll give you a hint on the subjects NOT part of the KDP stable of options. They are newsletters; PDF downloadable training documents or books, and content for our video YouTube channel.

You'll notice we've separated the contents into chapters with subchapters to better identify exact subject matter regarding the information you are reading. This is Chapter 4 and is about electronic publishing. It has subchapters (4A, 4B, etc.) to further explain how to treat different parts of the publishing process. For example, text and photographic requirements in an eBook differ a lot from those of a paperback edition.

Chapter 4-A: MS Word Text—Setup

As stated on the previous page, text requirements for an eBook are different than for a print-media book. What's different? The print-media book is destined for publication on a piece of paper (page) while an eBook will be read on a screen of some type. That screen might be on a small cell phone or on a large computer monitor; the options are many.

That means the first (and most important) item we'll discuss is setting up a Microsoft Word (2007) (MSW) template that has the ability to adjust its eBook content to fit any size screen. In other words, an eBook should respond to screen size like a cascading style sheet does on a present-day website—adjust to fill the page.

At this point in the e-publishing process, you have a couple of choices. One is to hire someone to format your MSW manuscript. We investigated that option early in our eBook career and discovered a book with multiple pictures like a fly-tying instructional eBook was expensive. The prices ranged from a $1.00 for a text-only page on up to more than $50.00 per page containing multiple pictures.

We thought that was too darned expensive. The other option was to do the formatting ourselves. This chapter gets us started down the do-it-yourself road. Note to the reader: In case our instructions are confusing OR your text-editing program is very different from ours, we've placed a pre-made Beatty's 36-Chapter MS Word EBook Template on our website for you to download and use with our compliments. If you use our template, be sure to change the important information like author's name, etc. and to add or delete chapters based on the size of your book. You'll find the template at the bottom of our homepage at www.btsflyfishing.com.

Before we start making the template understand we prefer typing our text and inserting our pictures DIRECTLY into our prepared template. In so doing, we are assembling the book as we go a chapter at a time.

Yes, it is possible to complete all of your typing in MSW then copy and paste it into the template. Whether you type directly into the template OR you cut and paste the **text**, the **pictures MUST** be added **AFTER** the text using the **Insert > Picture** command. **Do not try to make a manuscript first** (text and pictures together) then copy and paste them into the template. If you do so you are headed for disaster! Text first and pictures second **"inserted"** into the MSW template. Did we get your attention regarding the importance of **inserting** the pictures via the MSW menu process, **not** the drag & drop or cut & paste method? We hope so! Don't ask how we can speak on this subject with authority (experience). Just believe us when we offer the above warning.

With those thoughts in mind let's start building an MSW EBook Template. Complete instructions on using MS Word to set up an eBook **template** are on Amazon at https://kdp.amazon.com/en_US/help/topic/G200645680. A person would think the instructions for making a template on the Kindle site would be comprehensive. Unfortunately, we found their instructions left us scratching our heads. We hope you find following our directions in this subchapter a bit more helpful. We suggest saving the template you make from information in this subchapter. You'll be glad you did.

If you would rather use our template then you can skip this subchapter and go straight to the editing pictures for an eBook subchapter. **Before** you decide to skip forward though, we suggest skimming through this section and at least review the information on using the pilcrow (¶) near the end of this chapter. You'll need to understand it to finish the copy editing process outlined in that future subchapter.

This template is intended for use in a non-fiction, educational (fly-tying) eBook. Often when working with MSW the program has been used for many other projects. The result is "hidden" formatting that can really mess up a manuscript conversion to Kindle. The best way to eliminate that problem right from the start is to set the page style to "simple." To do so go to the **Change Styles** drop-down menu then select **Style Set > Simple**. Click on "Simple" as illustrated here in Figure 4-1.

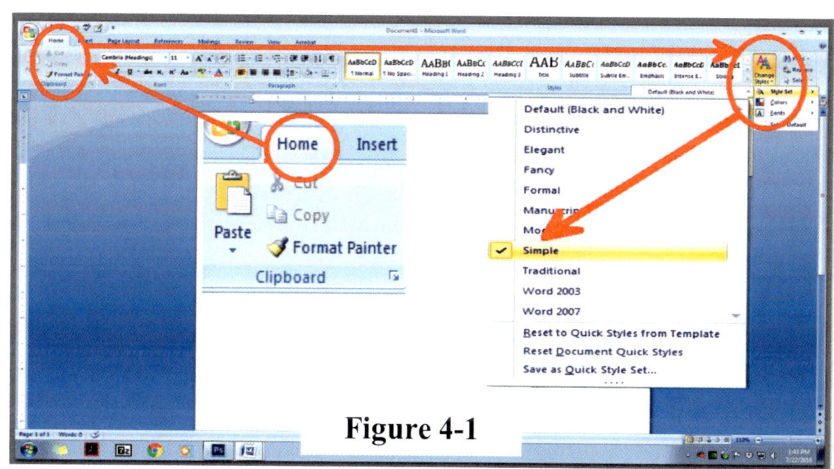

Figure 4-1

Before starting any of the other formatting let's set the page dimension to 5" by 8", which seems to be a size that works well with Kindle. We think it has something to do with the average size of a Kindle screen (device or app which is 6.25" by 8.33") but don't know that for sure. At the top of the MSW page click on the **Page Layout** tab in the menu bar, then click on the **Size** selection. The USA default size **Letter (8.5" x 11")** is probably already selected. Go to the bottom of the drop-down menu and click on **More Paper Sizes**. That brings up another menu where the middle tab is **Paper**. At the top of the drop-down menu adjust the sizes to **Width - 5"** and **Height – 8."** Click the **OK** tab at the bottom to exit the menu and set the page size.

Before we go any further let's save our page layout. It's IMPORTANT to save the newly started template as a **Word 97-2003 Document**, we'll name it "EBookTemplate." Why use that "older" setting? Because some of the newer MSW document settings do not play nice with the Kindle publishing process. Once saved the complete file should read "EBookTemplate.doc." If the file ends with an extension of ".docx," the "x" indicates the file was saved as a newer, unwanted file format. Go back and redo the **File > Save > Word 97-2003 Document** process so the file ends with the ".doc" extension.

Next, we'll select the default font for use throughout the whole book. Here we'll change the default font to Cambria (Headings). Select the **Home** tab then select **Cambria (Headings)** with a font size of **11**. That selection will produce a highlighted square around the **Normal** box in the **Word Quick Access Toolbar**. The other font selections you'll be using for this template is the **Title** box (**Cambria 26**) and **Subtitle** box (**Cambria 14**). We've placed arrows pointing at "Cambria (Headings) font selection box, Normal, Title, and Subtitle." See Figure 4-2 below:

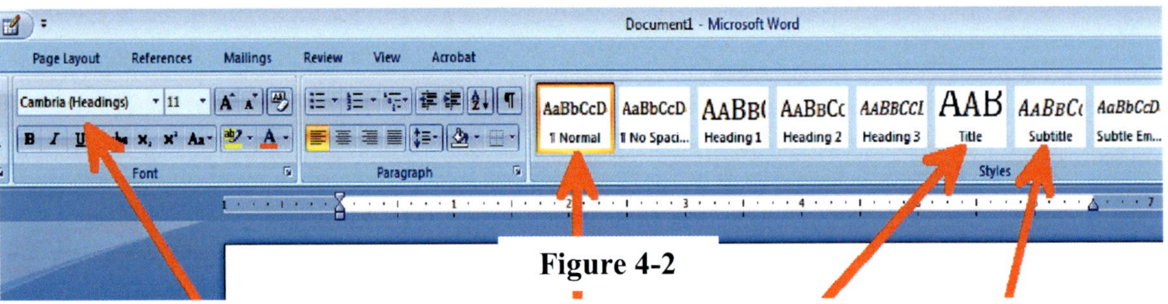

Figure 4-2

Setting up the line spacing and paragraph indent is our next consideration. It's simple. We like to space our text so the lines are not jammed tight again each other. Therefore we space them using the 1.15 option in the drop-down menu. Using that same drop-down menu we'll make our selections so MSW automatically places an extra space between the paragraphs. We DO NOT INDENT our paragraphs because although that indent works just fine with text, that formatting option hidden away in your document can cause some of the photographs you'll insert later to not fit on the screen.

We like to "center" the text on our "Title Page" but that is up to you. NOTE regarding text: When selecting the font to use in our manuscript we selected Cambria because it is near the top of the selection options on our version of MSW and we know it will traverse the Kindle publishing process with no formatting problems. THIS IS IMPORTANT: When a customer reads your book THEY select the font and size they want based on their personal needs and what is available on their particular Kindle, tablet, Smartphone, or computer. What you select for your template really makes little difference other than using a font Kindle likes. That's why we use Cambria as our base font; Kindle likes it and it's near the top of the MSW font menu. Also, this is a good time to explain how to check for page breaks and ALL other formatting information in your text. We use the "pilcrow" (¶) to turn on and off that information. You'll find the ¶ (pilcrow) under the **Home** tab in the **Paragraph** section as indicated here in Figure 4-3.

Figure 4-3

This is a good time for you to open any one of your MSW documents and use the pilcrow to check your formatting. Turn it off and on a few times. Notice each space has a dot to indicate there is a space between words. If you accidentally put more than one space between words you'll quickly see that formatting error so you can correct it. Also, a pilcrow is placed at the end of each paragraph so you can easily identify when you have an unwanted line in your text. We have used MSW for many years and never knew what the pilcrow was. After using it for the last couple of years, we don't know how we ever managed without it! You may find it equally helpful with your writing. Now let's open a blank MSW document to set up a title page.

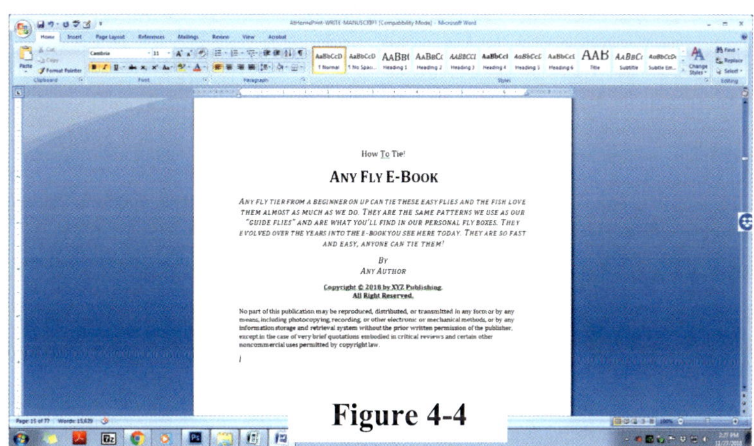

Figure 4-4

Figure 4-4 is a screen capture of the title page you'll find waiting for you at www.btsflyfishing.com should you elect to use it. IF you'd rather make your own it is quite easy. Just open a blank document using the settings we've already established and place the following text to build the page. "How to Tie!" = **Cambria 14—Normal**, "Book Title" = **Cambria 26, Bold—Title**, "Subtitle text" = **Cambria 14, Italic—Subtitle**, "Copyright date—publisher" **Cambria 11, Bold—Normal**, "Reproduction-copyright's text" **Cambria 11—Normal**.

At this point, it's important to insert a "break" so the Title Page stays on a separate page in our subsequent Kindle eBook. Figure 4-5 shows how to do this. Click on the **Insert** tab then click again on **Page Break** or you can just press **Control + Return** on the keyboard.

Figure 4-5

Chapter 4-B: Table of Contents

We like to put a Table of Contents (TOC) on the page after the Title Page so the reader can easily navigate throughout the book. Unfortunately, the Table of Contents is where the confusion often begins. Why? Because it appears in the eBook immediately AFTER the title page and BEFORE the body of the eBook. Unfortunately, the chapters are part of the body-of-the-Book and MUST be in place for the TOC to have a destination direction toward which to navigate.

Let's start eliminating the confusion by defining "navigation" within a Microsoft Word (MSW) document. The correct way to use the TOC to navigate is via the (MSW) **Control + Click** mouse function. While hovering over a TOC chapter number with the **Control Key** depressed, the reader **Clicks** the left mouse key to navigate to the chapter selected via the hover method.

What's equally important, the destination **chapter title** MUST BE FORMATED using the **Title** font selected from the **Word Quick Access Toolbar** discussed previously in the center of page 28. If a font other than Title is used the TOC will not function as a navigation tool and also it will not "UPDATE" to the new text if changes are made to the chapter title.

All of this may be as clear as mud so on the next two pages we'll build a TOC, two sample chapters, and then update the TOC to reflect those two chapters. We'll start by using the new page that is automatically inserted whenever we execute a "Page Break" as we did in Figure 4-5 at the bottom of the previous page. With this new page open we'll select **Title** from the **Word Quick Access Toolbar** and type the words "Table of Con-

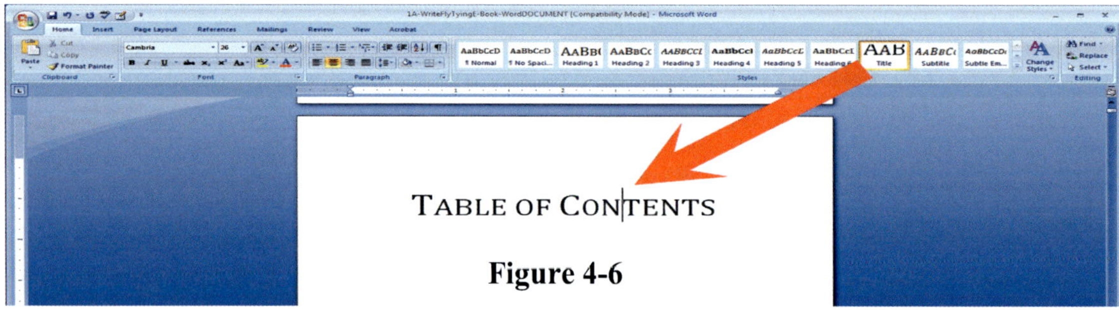

Figure 4-6

tents centered near the top of the page (Figure 4-6). The page is blank except for the Table of Contents title at the top. We used the "Title" TOC text because we'll need it later when we build a return to the **Table of Contents** hyperlink at the end of each chapter. It's purpose is to help readers navigate back and forth in the book.

Upon placing a "page break" after the TOC title we'll go ahead and build two sample chapter TEMPLATE pages illustrated in Figure 4-7. We used "Title" font for the chapter titles and "Normal" font for the body text. Also notice the "Return Table of Contents" hyperlink followed by a page break. We turned on the "pilcrow" to identify our formatting and page breaks. When we add or amend the text, the page break (thus chapter break) just keeps getting pushed down until we reach the end of a chapter. You might wonder how long the pages are in an eBook; the answer is "one" displayed using as many screens as it needs AND the screen size can change based on the size of the computer, Smartphone, Kindle reader, etc. being used. Crazy, isn't it?

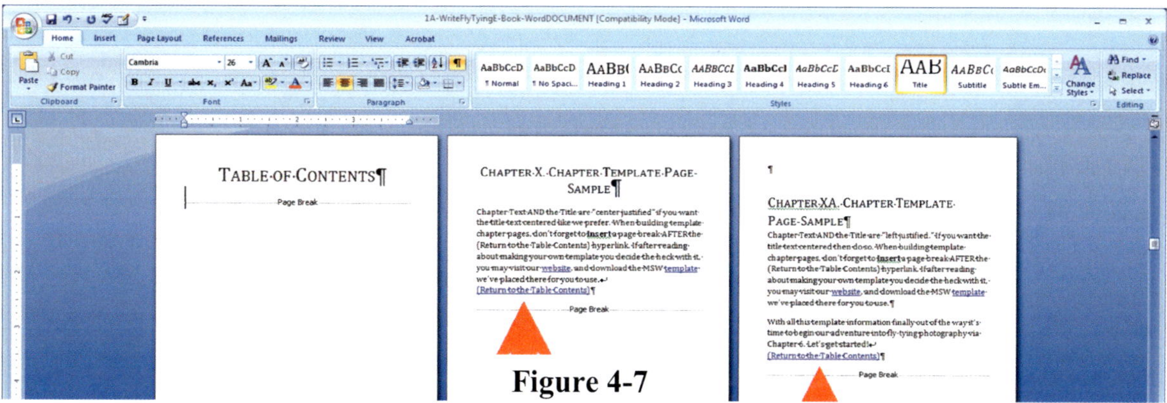

Figure 4-7

Now it's time to go back to the TOC page and update it to reflect the two chapter template titles we just finished adding. To update the TOC titles, please note we have a "curser" on the left below the TOC title AND in front of the page break. To add a TOC in place of our cursor we'll select the **Reference** tab then click on **Table of Contents** in the menu below. That option brings up a drop-down menu. We'll navigate to the very bottom where we'll select **Insert Table of Contents**. This brings up another menu where we'll make four selections. (**1**) Uncheck the **Show Page Numbers** box: (**2**) Be sure to check **Use hyperlinks instead of page numbers**: (**3**) Change the **Show Levels** drop-down menu to **1**: and (**4**) Click the **OK** button.

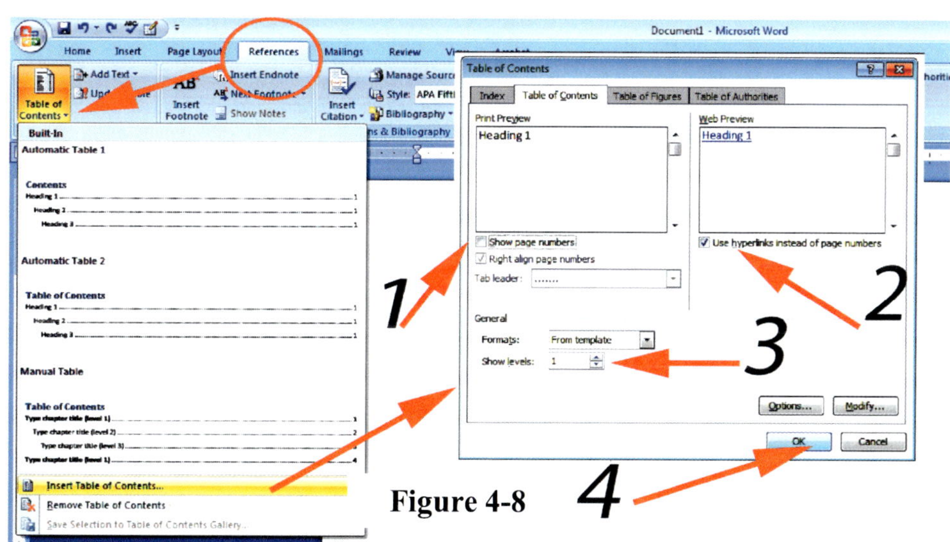

Figure 4-8

Remember the curser on the left below the TOC title in Figure 4-7 on page 31? It will look the same as before we "set up" the TOC in Figure 4-8 but that Table of Contents is there in the background waiting to be brought up-to-date with the rest of the manuscript template. To accomplish that update, click the **References** tab then follow the red arrow to **Update Table** selection. Click it and the Table of Contents below in Figure 4-9 appears like magic.

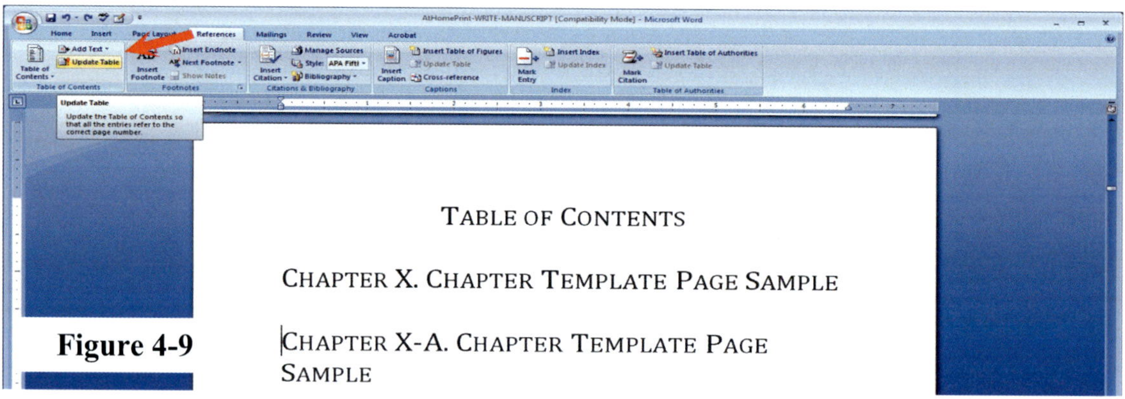

Figure 4-9

Above is an example of a two-chapter TOC but you can build as many chapters as you wish. As you **insert** chapter pages with titles just go back to the TOC page and select the **References > Update Table** option to make changes or corrections. Remember, you DO NOT change the Table of Contents information by typing on that page. You BUILD the chapter title page first then execute a **References > Update Table** command.

Remember the "**Return Table of Contents**" words we discussed on page 30 that are positioned at the end of the chapters. It is an easy way to hyperlink back to the TOC after reaching the end of a chapter; it's much simpler than scrolling all the way back. Very few authors use this tool but we think is helpful to the reader. Figure 4-10 illustrates the process. First place your cursor where you want the hyperlink. Select the **Insert** tab then click on the **Hyperlink** icon (or use **Control + K**) to access the **Insert Hyperlink** menu. From it, click the left-hand **Place in this Document** tab. At the top of that menu, use the **Text to Display** space and type the words "Return Table of Contents." Select **Table of Contents** under the **Headings** section, click **OK**, and your hyperlink is done.

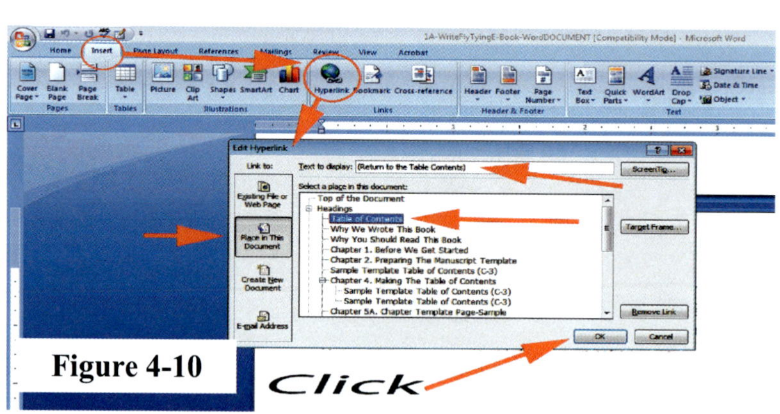

Figure 4-10

Chapter 4-C: Editing Pictures for Kindle

Editing the pictures you have stored in your fresh-from-the-camera (OOC) directory is where things get a bit "dicey" when converting your Microsoft Word (MSW) manuscript to Kindle. First MSW likes a manuscript written on a PC to have pictures inserted into it that are 96 pixels per inch (PPI) if the document is destined for publication on a digital screen. On the other hand, MSW likes the same manuscript written on a MAC to have pictures inserted that are 72 PPI. The 72 PPI is thankfully not a mandatory requirement. Why? This is the "dicey" part we mentioned above.

Kindle wants its picture uploads to it to be 96 PPI. If they don't meet that requirement then Kindle will change them so they ARE 96 PPI. You may be thinking, "So what!" Here's why! Kindle will not accept a picture file any larger than 128 KB in size and if you send it a larger file it (Kindle) will change it? A 96 PPI file is 1.34 times larger than the same 72 PPI file. If you use a MAC and edit your picture file so it is 128 KB at 72 PPI Kindle will change it to 96 PPI. That increases the file size from 128 KB to about 170 KB. We hate to tell you this but Kindle won't like that one darned bit and IT will reduce the size down to 128 KB. You may or may not like what their random computer "change" does to your picture. So! We suggest you MAC users either edit your picture files to about 72 percent of 128 KB or save them as 96 KB files in the first place.

Right now you PC users are probably feeling kind of superior. Well, don't! Kindle always messes with your file size a bit so it's a good idea you do not push the envelope. Edit your picture files so they do not exceed 115 KB. Then you know you'll not have a Kindle machine undoing your post-processing work.

The bottom line for both MAC and PC users: Edit your pictures so they don't exceed 115 KB at 96 PPI. Microsoft Word for MAC may not like the 96 PPI but just override any messages that pop up on your screen during manuscript preparation. Your Kindle conversion will be a more pleasant experience.

Editing Pictures

We use Photoshop to edit all of our pictures. If you use other programs then you'll need to figure out how to convert our instructions to fit your particular editing software.

We've had numerous other authors tell us that Kindle tends to "read" pictures edited in Photoshop or Photoshop Elements better than those using other programs. We don't know if that's true or not. Photoshop is the only program we've used since getting our first digital camera in 2004. We have no experience with any of the other programs.

For illustration purposes, we'll be using the picture of the Adams Parachute captured using the Nikon Coolpix 995 from Chapter 2.

We always keep our eBook photographs in two different folders. The first folder is for the original picture (OOC) and the second is for the file when it is ready to **insert** into the manuscript (WEB). Notice in Figure 4-11, we've identified the two folders as "FT-EBookPix-OOC" and the other is FT-EBookPix-WEB. You may want to use different directory "identifiers" but they are what works for us.

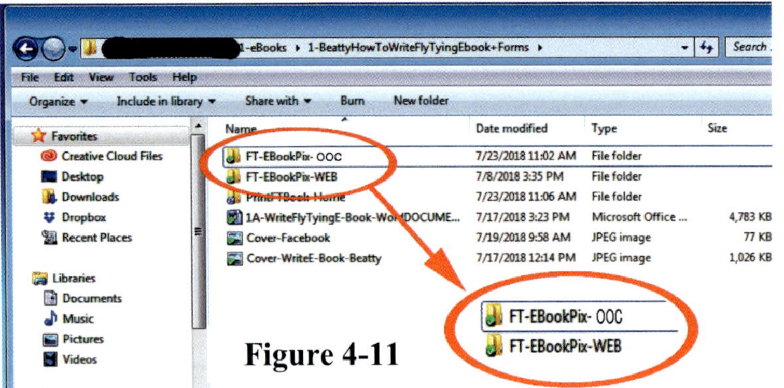

Figure 4-11

Now let's start the multi-step editing process. We really recommend you do the steps in the SAME sequence we suggest to ensure the best quality. Let's start by opening the picture file in Photoshop. Because we are using a JPG file straight from the Nikon 995 it has already been processed and sharpened based on the camera's menu settings.

Once we've added any additional minor changes and we are satisfied no other corrections are needed we'll save the file for the web. To do so we go to the **File** drop-down menu and select **Save for Web** (**Shift, Control,** and **Alt+ S**). Figure 4-12 comes up with options we'll need to change. In number **1** select **JPG**, number **2** select **medium**, number **3** select a **Quality** setting of **40**, number **4** select **sRGB**, and number **5** execute a **Save** command. That brings up the **Save option** screen where we select the directory (**FT-EBookPix-WEB** = 1.) and change the name by adding "**Web**" to it (Figure 4-13).

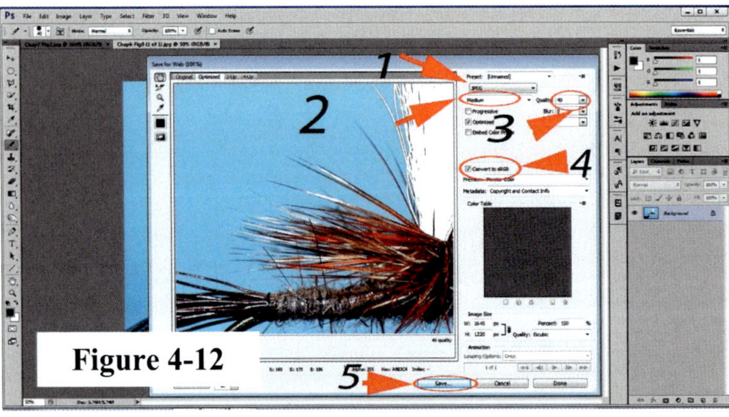

Figure 4-12

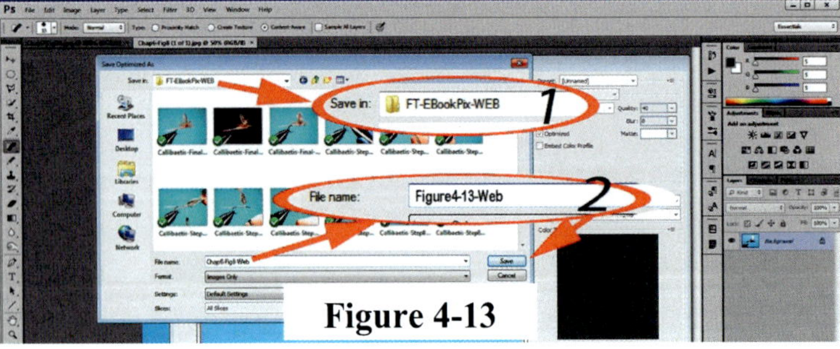

Figure 4-13

At this point, we are halfway to the finish line. The last couple of steps will reduce the picture file from about 150 KB down to the goal of 115 KB at 96 PPI or LESS. First, we must close the original OOC file we were working on (remember, we don't want to copy over it) and open the NEW file Figure4-13-Web that has already been reduced in size and SAVED to a separate directory, FT-EBookPix-WEB. The original out-of-camera (OOC) file is now safe in its storage directory where it will remain until we again use it to produce a print-media file in Chapter 5.

In the illustration, we've opened the picture file that was saved to the WEB directory in Photoshop and selected the menu item **Image > Image Size**. In that screen, we changed **Width** to **5 inches** (that automatically changes the height to about **3.5 inches**) and then adjust the **Resolution** to **96 PPI** as indicated in Figure 4-14.

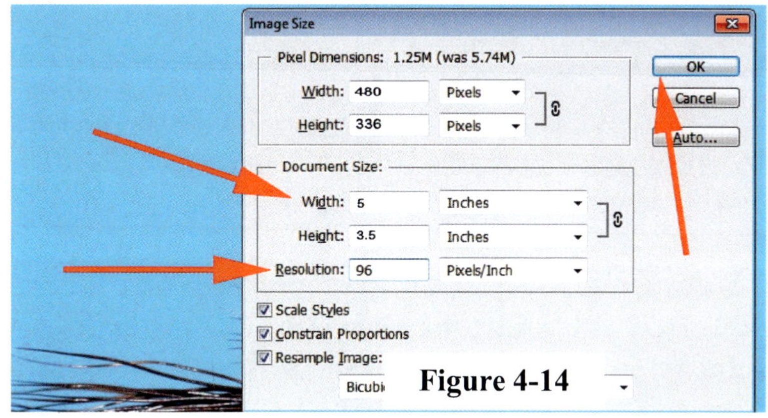

Figure 4-14

Above, when we click on the **OK** button in Figure 4-14 the next option is to execute a **File > Save As** where we finish reducing the size. In the screen in Figure 4-14A we changed the **Quality** from **12 – High** down to **5 – Medium** as indicated by the circle. Clicking **OK** finishes the downsizing process. The file is ready for Kindle!

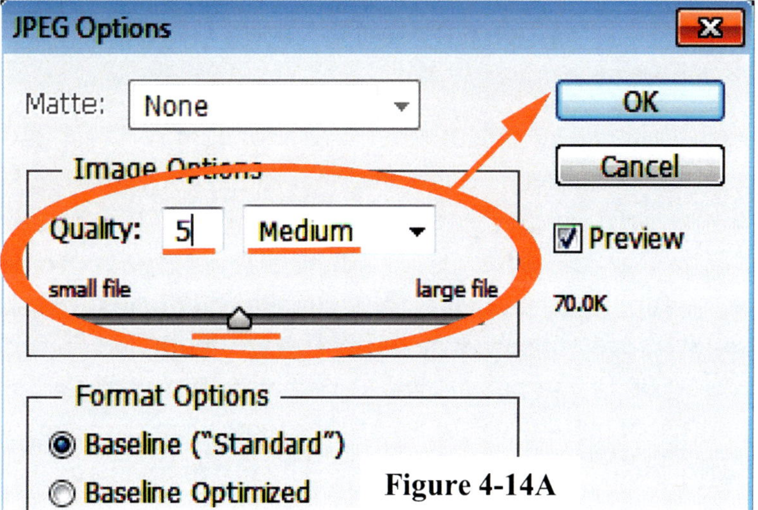

Figure 4-14A

The Parachute Adams is ready to insert into THIS manuscript. The original file was 8 MB (megabytes, million bytes) when we downloaded it from the camera. The edited version for Kindle is now 55 KB (kilobytes, thousand bytes) and it still looks very good on the screen. We'll use the **Insert > Picture** command to insert the picture. We'll review inserting pictures and other manuscript items in the next chapter. For now, enjoy the edited Parachute Adams on the next page knowing the 5" x 3.5" x 96 PPI will render a clear, sharp image on a Kindle device or computer screen.

Figure 4-15

Before we exit this subchapter on picture editing we'll leave you with a few random tidbits of information regarding pictures for Kindle. They are:
**The smallest picture allowed is 300 x 400 pixels...
**A full-size page = 1200 x 1800 pixels...
On a Kindle device or on a Kindle computer APP the machine will adjust a "too large" picture to fit the screen rather than cut it off as long as the file size is **less than 128 KB...
**A manuscript for Kindle MUST be smaller than 50 MB...
**We manage to keep our manuscript sizes to less than 5 MB using the editing tips herein...
We've found using JPG for all of our illustrations works well for us. If we have a line drawing to publish, we just change the JPG picture to black & white then use **Images > Adjustments > Levels in Photoshop to make it look as sharp as possible...

Chapter 4-D: Text, Pictures, Copy Editing

We reviewed setting up Microsoft Word (MSW) text in Chapter 4A but one item we didn't cover is very important. That item is how text and pictures work together or don't work together. In the case of MSW, it easily accomplishes functions that drive Kindle crazy. So what drives Kindle crazy? **Important:** MSW WILL NOT WORK with text wrapping around a picture considered normal with all print media. For those of you who are not sure what "word wrap" might be, Figure 4-16 is an example while Figure 4-16A is a sample of "inline text and photographs." As readers, we see word wrap so often we don't realize it until we read a Kindle eBook where text and photographs MUST be **in line** with each other. The top of this page is an example of word wrap.

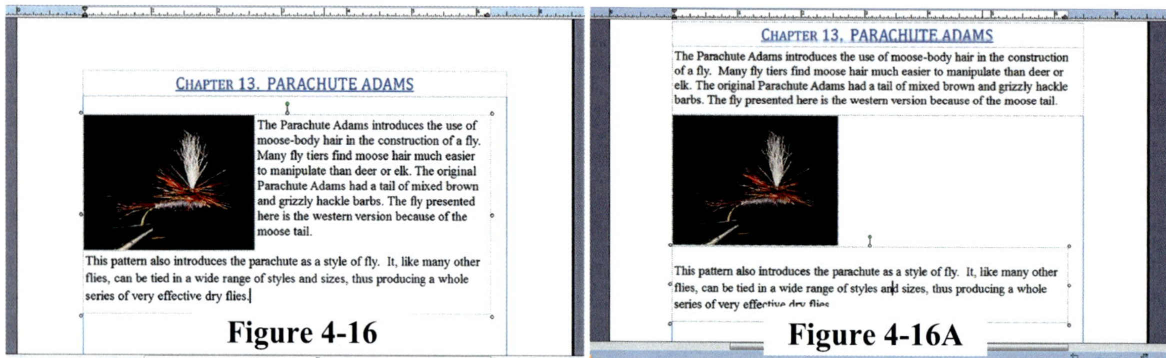

Figure 4-16 Figure 4-16A

This situation may seem crazy but it's just the way Kindle functions in our present, 2018 world. We've heard "rumors" the company is working on that problem (and several others) with the goal of making changes sometime in the next "few" years. We heard that promise **more** than a few years ago and it still has not changed. No matter when KDP gets to the problem, today you'll have to accept the fact your text and photographs must be **in line** with each other. Who knows what the future will bring.

Even though we must accept the situation as it is today; there are a couple of ways to compensate for the inline requirement. We'll get to them in a few paragraphs but for now, it might be a good idea to first learn the proper (and only) way to **insert** a picture in your manuscript. Notice the word "**insert**" in the last sentence. It's a critical word as you'll soon learn. ***A KDP Rule:*** *NEVER drag & drop OR copy & paste a picture into your manuscript UNLESS it has already been* ***inserted*** *at an earlier location IN the SAME manuscript.*

Once your picture is edited and saved to the WEB directory with a file size of 115 KB at 96 PPI (or less), we are ready to bring it and the manuscript together. To properly INSERT a JPG file in MSW, click the menu tabs **Insert > Picture**. Doing so brings up the menu options in Figure 4-17.

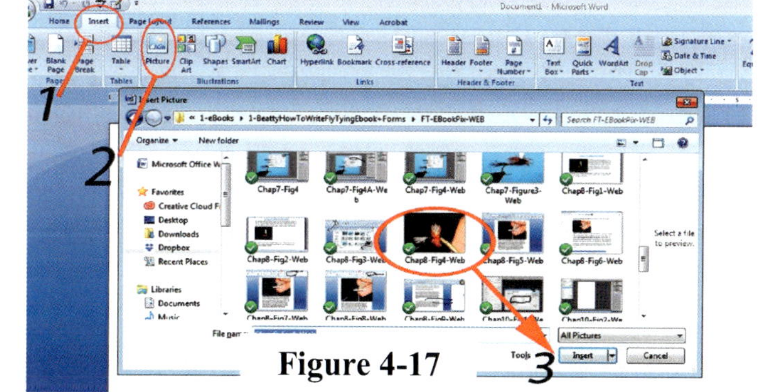

Figure 4-17

Figure 4-17 only shows us how to access the picture in preparation to **insert** it into our text but it leaves out one important thing – the spacing between the text and the picture. Let's pretend for a moment we are inserting Figure 4-18 as the last step in a six-step instructional series. In **Step 6** below and directly under the picture instead of using fly tying instructional text, we'll share with you the process we use to get the picture **locked to the text**. Be sure to **READ** the information AFTER the words "**Step 6**" to see how we locked the text and picture together.

Figure 4-18

Step 6: We like to place our step-by-step pictures directly above the text explaining what is happening and left justified. To accomplish it, first, type the text for the particular fly-tying step. Next, place the cursor to the **left** of the "**S**" in the word **Step**, hold down the **Shift Key**, and hit **Enter** once to place a space **above** the text. Now press the **up arrow** key once so the cursor is in that space located directly above the word **Step**.

Last we follow the instructions outlined in Figure 4-17 – **Insert > Picture**, select the picture and click **OK.** As you can see the picture is above the word "Step" and because we used the **shift + enter + up arrow** command the text and picture are "tied" to each other. Note: You can position the picture AFTER the text by placing the cursor at the end of it then press **shift + enter** once. That positions the cursor directly below the text then use the **Insert > Picture** process. If for some reason you want the picture to be by itself then be sure to have a space placed both above AND below the inserted picture. Then it's free-floating and not locked to any text.

Once we've placed the picture and it is left justified like in the sample step-by-step on page 37., you've probably noticed the void in your manuscript to the right of the picture produced by the inline document option explained earlier in this chapter. It's not terrible but it's a bit distracting. We have a couple of methods to make it less obvious or completely disappear.

The simplest method is to "center" justify your pictures instead of "left" justifying them. In so doing, the big void in one spot is less noticeable when it's not all in the same place. It's important to understand when "center justifying" a picture that you MUST unlock the photo from the text by inserting a space between the two. If you don't "break the lock," the text will also center justify. Note: We DO NOT recommend "right" justifying your pictures. We've never done it but should you decide to try let us know how it works out for you. Our contact information is at www.btsflyfishing.com.

Another way to compensate for the void is to "adjust" your picture to fill a good portion of the space. That sounds easy and quite frankly it is once you know the trick but we spent the better part of two years figuring out what we'll share with you in the next few paragraphs.

Early in the book, when we set up the page size for our eBook template it was 5" wide x 8" high. Also, we often save our pictures for Kindle so they are 8" wide by 6" high at 96 PPI if the file size doesn't exceed 115 Kb. If you take a look at the two sets of measurements you'll soon see the picture is too wide for the page. Right? Something has to happen and it definitely does! It is readily evident if you review Figure 4-19 and Figure 4-20.

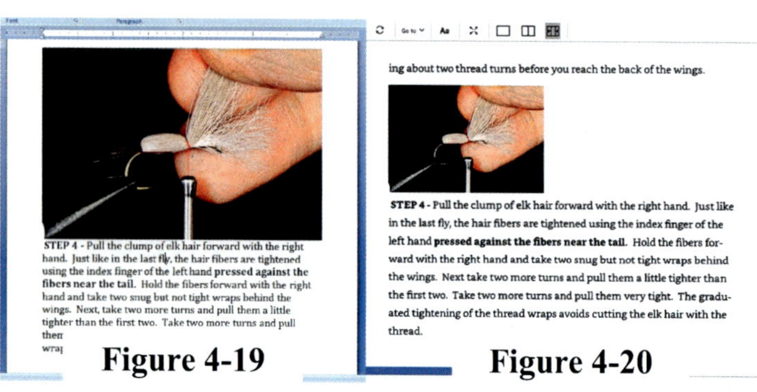

Figure 4-19 Figure 4-20

The first picture is how it appears in our MSW document and the other is how it appears on our computer's Kindle APP screen once it is published as an eBook. Wow! What happened? The picture in our MSW document covers most of the page while the one on our Kindle APP only covers about half. The answer is simple but we had a heck of a time figuring it out. You see, MSW recognizes you are trying to put a larger picture on a 5" page and it reduces the photograph's DISPLAY size so it will fit on your computer screen (minus any margins). In our case, it DISPLAYS the original 8" picture at 4" so it will fit when you view your document. Isn't MSW nice to do that for us? It keeps the full-size picture in the background and displays a smaller version on the screen. See Figure 4-21 below and note the circle around the picture size menu. The problem raises its ugly head when you publish to Kindle and end up with a picture that only covers half of the Kindle screen. If you've forgotten, look back at Figure 4-20 on page 38 to see the picture size in relation to the full screen on the computer Kindle APP.

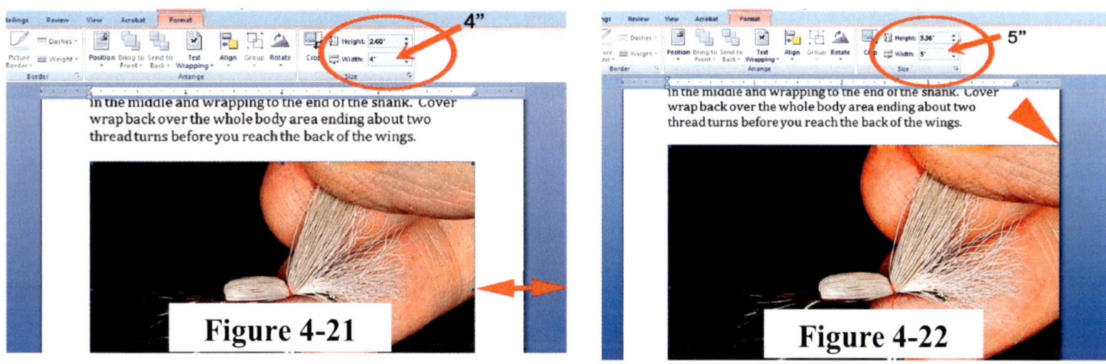

Figure 4-21

Figure 4-22

The fix is fairly straightforward. Just double-click on any picture in the MSW document you feel should look bigger than a half-page wide and change the size from 4" to a bigger number. In Figure 4-22 we've changed the picture size from 4" to 5." Now when we click one more time on the picture MSW overrides the original DISPLAY size and replaces it with another display picture sized for the new width (5"). Unfortunately, your new display picture disappears off the right side of the screen.

Now, what can we do? Don't worry, when you publish to Kindle it will use the new size (5") you selected UNLESS that display size is bigger than the Kindle screen can handle. In that case, Kindle automatically reduces the picture so it will FIT the FULL screen (minus margins) being used at any given time – Smartphone, tablet, Kindle, or computer. Just in case you are wondering, that ability to adjust the picture (and text) size is similar to a "Cascading Style Sheet (CSS) used on most web pages. CSS allows viewing web pages on multiple sized digital displays while still filling its screen.

There is one other way to change picture size and it is during the first step of the publishing process when we convert the MSW manuscript to an HTML file. When we get to that point in the book we'll bring it to your attention. We've found resizing the picture now at the time we insert it much easier to do than when we are in the middle of another process – HTML conversion and publishing the manuscript. The option is yours.

Copy editing your work is a very important process but it only takes a few sentences to discuss it. We find that fact really ironic but in reality, your text, syntax usage, etc. is either right or wrong! End of story! Regarding copy editing, you basically have two choices. You can do the copy editing yourself or hire a professional to do it. The first is less expensive and the second is not.

For us, we've found using a free program called Grammarly (app.grammarly.com/ - download page) to work well for us. In addition to that program, the fact Gretchen is a former English teacher and we both have ten years experience as magazine editors allows us to do our own copy editing with a minimal number of mistakes. You have to see what works for you.

Is our system perfect? No it's not but Grammarly really does a fairly good job and the price is right. Also, we use Google to help clarify information so hopefully we don't make too many mistakes. We have two mistakes in this paragraph and Grammarly found them both. See Figure 4-23 where we show the program installed in our version of MSW.

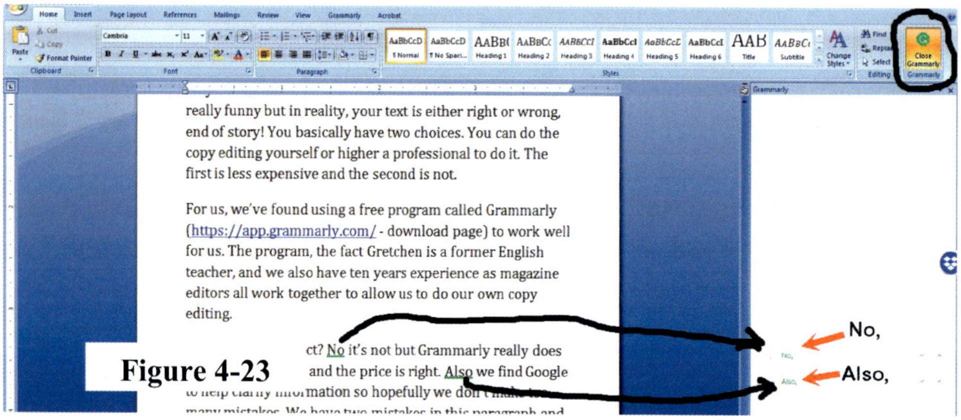

Figure 4-23

Some copy editors (the real people) we know will "read" the manuscript text backward starting with the last paragraph, then the next to the last, and so on while working their way to the start of a document. Reading the manuscript in this manner helps (only helps) keep your mind from "putting or changing" words in a sentence.

Another option is to read the manuscript out loud to your self because saying each word tends to stop the mind from inserting or changing words that are not there. EX: "I'll read me manuscript from back to front." In the previous sentence, the mind will often convert the word "me" to "my" and go on just as if "my" was the word there all along. Out loud reading tends to reduce that problem – at least it does for us. Note: We each read the manuscript out loud (once per person) then complete two more "reads" each. We'll complete a couple of final edits followed by a spelling and formatting verification just before we convert the manuscript to HTML.

You'll have to find out what process works best for you; there is always the option of hiring a professional. We don't think a fly-tying book is anywhere close to rocket science and as such isn't important enough to hire a professional copy editor.

You also have one last option to check your work and Kindle does it for you as part of the publishing process. It will be the section where we are given the option of viewing the document as it will appear on a Kindle (computer screen, tablet, or Smartphone). It will tell you if you have any spelling errors.

Sample Booklet: We debated at length whether to include a sample book/chapter thinking it might be a waste of your time. We finally concluded it did have value and might even make clear some of the items we reviewed up to this point in the book. The sample booklet we include here is a single pattern eBook we wrote and published to test our "new" discoveries regarding picture sizing.

Notice the three red arrows. Those are locations where we double clicked on a picture and changed its size from the default 4" to a new size based on how we wanted the picture to display on a Kindle device. The first red arrow is pointing at a picture we wanted to display across the full Kindle screen so we sized it slightly larger than our 5" template page. We also "center justified" the picture so it would be in the middle of a large 27" computer monitor if a person was so inclined to view it on that size of device.

We resized and/or centered three other pictures including the bottom left two with red arrows. This picture is not here for you readers to learn a fly-tying lesson. Its only purpose will become evident when we make a book cover and execute the publishing process starting with the next subchapter on page 42. We needed an actual book to better illustrate the more important parts of the Kindle uploading process.

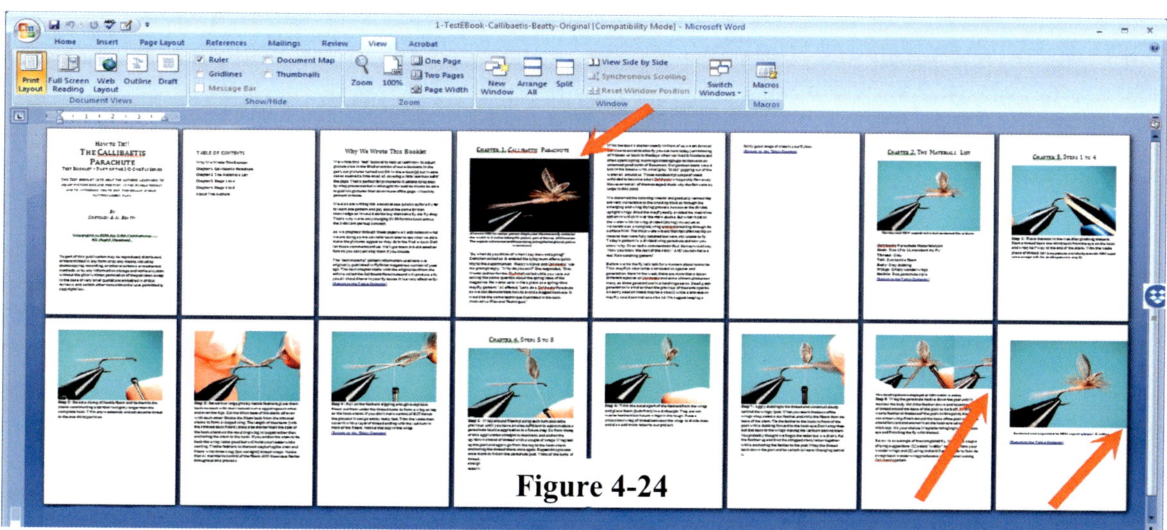

Figure 4-24

Chapter 4-E: The eBook Cover

An eBooks' cover is the most important part of its success even though it's often only used once. When might that be? It's when a potential customer is deciding whether or not to purchase it. Therefore, this is the only time we really focus on a high-resolution file and that starts with the template.

You have many choices regarding your book's cover. You can hire a professional to design it, use a pre-made template from the Kindle website (https://kdp.amazon.com/en_US/) or make it yourself.

We've never hired a person to design a fly-tying eBook cover but did check Google to see what options might be available. We entered "design cover for eBook" in the search engine and got over 58 million hits. The first selection took us to a page where you could get a cover designed for as little as $5.00 on up to $500.00. We didn't check any further than the first page of that particular website. You can explore this option further if you wish.

Your next option is to use one of Kindle Direct Publishing (KDP) templates to design your book cover. Here is a link (https://kdp.amazon.com/en_US/help/topic/G201113520) to the KDP cover page where you will find written instructions and a YouTube video to get you started.

We felt the unique nature of a fly-tying eBook warranted making our own. None of the templates we saw worked for us so we've used Photoshop to design all of our eBook covers but you can also use Microsoft Word (MSW), Microsoft Publisher (MSP) or any one of many other programs. No matter which program you may utilize just be sure to use these dimensions. They are 1410 pixels wide by 2250 pixels tall by 300 PPI or 4.7" by 7.5" by 300 PPI. Notice we used 300 PPI for this template rather than the 96 PPI we used for photographs and screen captures. Remember, the cover is one instance we want a high-resolution file. Note: The high-resolution cover you submit for publication is actually split into two files. One is attached as a low-resolution cover for the actual Kindle book you see on your Kindle device. The high-resolution cover file you submit is used on the Amazon website to illustrate your book in their books-for-sale library, hoping to attract many customers.

In case you are interested we'll show how to set up a blank cover template in Photoshop. Start by clicking on **File > New** then enter 4.7 inches in the **Width** box; 7.5 inches in the **Height** box; and 300 PPI in the **Resolution** box. If you wish you may use the **Control+N** keyboard shortcut. No matter which method you use, the screen will look something like Figure 4-25 on the next page.

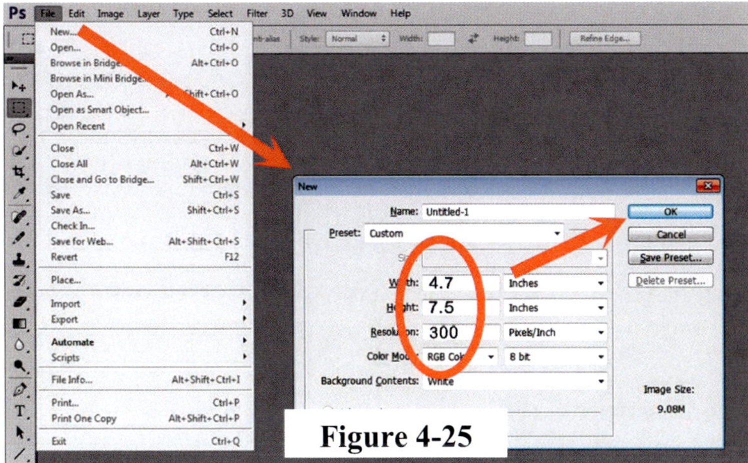

Figure 4-25

When you click on the **OK** button your template magically appears. Execute a **File > Save As** command to keep this template safe for future use. We saved our template in a JPG format with a file name of "E-BookCoverTemplate.jpg."

Figure 4-26

We've used our template many times over the years to design covers for our eBooks and you may want to as well. Below is the cover we designed for the sample booklet in Chapter 9. All we did for this simple design was to add a background layer, a title layer, and **Insert**ed a photograph layer to complete the cover illustrated in Figure 4-27.

Figure 4-27

Once you've created your cover, be sure to save it as a JPG file. In the case of the cover in Figure 4-27, we saved it as CallibaetisParachute.jpg in the SAME directory as our manuscript file. Saving it to the same directory makes finding it easier when you are in the middle of the publishing process. Go to the next page to start that process.

Chapter 4-F: Preparing for Publication

Once the draft manuscript and cover are done, we like to let them sit for a couple of days. Each of us will then execute another and final proofread. After those two proofreads, we perform a final spell, Grammarly, and formatting check using the pilcrow (¶) to verify spacing and page breaks. We reviewed the pilcrow at the top of page 29 in Chapter 4 in case it's one of the sections you skipped. It's a very helpful editing tool!

Now it's time to PREPARE our edited **sample** *Callibaetis* Parachute manuscript for publication. Please follow these instructions in the same order we offer them so your Kindle publishing experience will be positive. First, we'll go into the "TestBook-ParaCallibaetis" directory (book illustrated at the bottom of page 41) and ADD a new directory called "CallibaetisParachute-HTMLWeb," Figure 4-28.

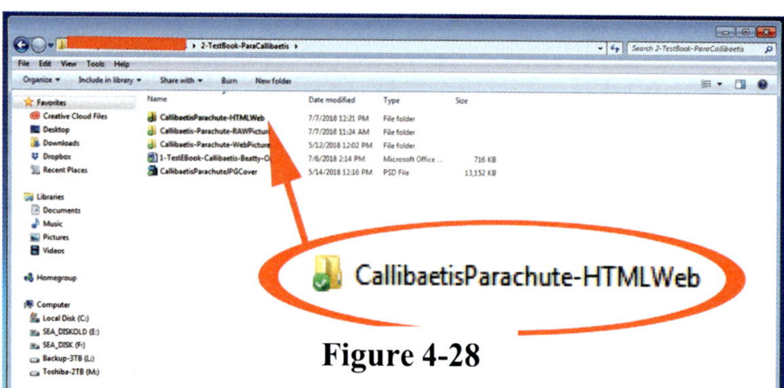

Figure 4-28

Now that we have the empty HTML directory we must open our MSW *Callibaetis* Parachute document and convert it to an HTML file. To do so in MSW, click on **File > Save As > Web Page Filtered** from the drop-down menu and save it to the new HTML directory. After clicking the **OK** button the save command produces an HTML file of the document with an associated folder (called CallibaetisParachuteBooklet-Final_files) with the pictures inside of it as illustrated in Figure 4.29

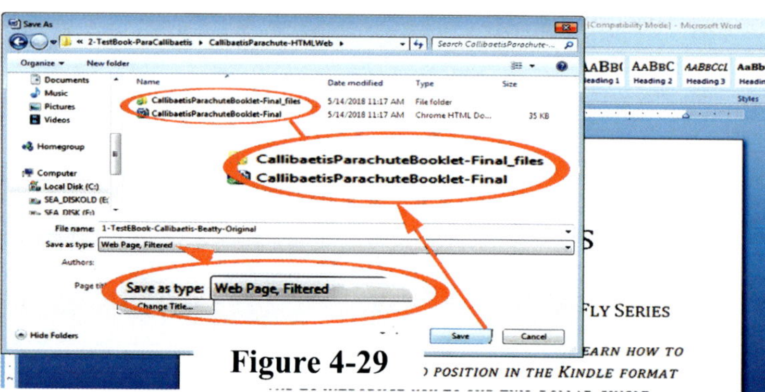

Figure 4-29

This is the LAST time you can adjust the size of any pictures. We'll open the HTML file and let you see what it looks like including the pictures sized as they will appear in the final Kindle document. We resize them the same way we did in our MSW manuscript, double-click on the picture and change the dimension to the size we wish.

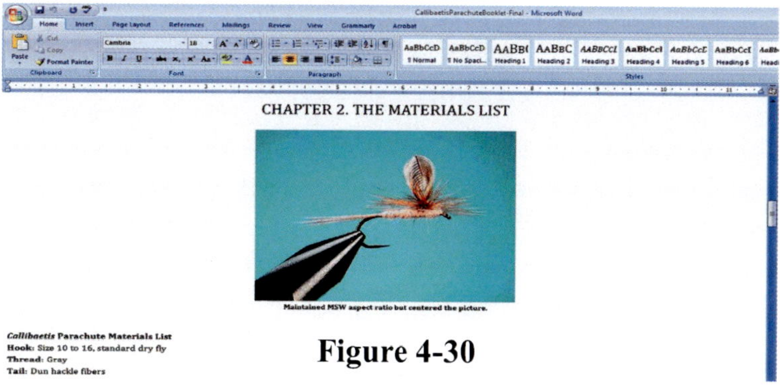

Figure 4-30

See Figure 4-30 to view the HTML version of the document with the resized picture. Note how small the text is in relation to the picture then compare it the same text/picture in your MSW eBook document. The difference is based on the screen width. In this HTML version, you are viewing the complete computer screen page. When you are viewing the MSW document you are seeing a 5"-wide screen, the page width established when we made the MSW eBook template earlier in Chapter 4A.

Before these files can be uploaded to KDP, the PICTURE directory AND the HTML file MUST be compressed to make one ZIP file which will be **imported** into the KDP process at the appropriate place. To execute the ZIP process we go into the HTML directory, highlight the **picture directory** AND the **HTML file**, and right-click them to bring up the ZIP option menu. Select the **Send to > Compressed (zipped) folder** illustrated in Figure 4-31.

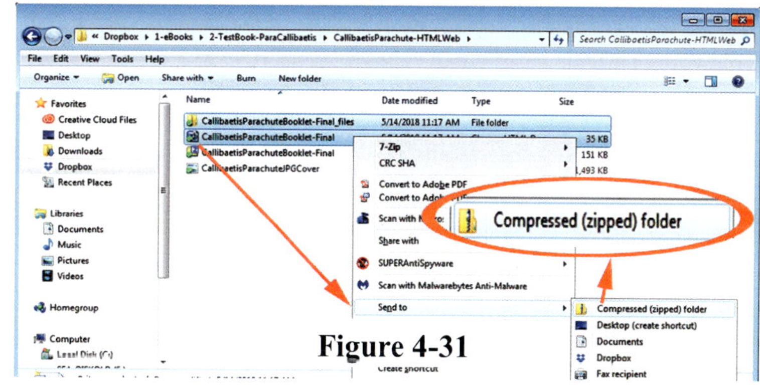

Figure 4-31

Click the **Compressed (zipped) folder** option and the zipped file is immediately created. It is the file used during the KDP publishing process. Notice in Figure 4-32 we also moved the JPG cover file over to this directory so it is with the "ZIP" file. We've learned over the years that even though they are placed in the KDP publishing template at different times, it is really helpful to have both together where they are easy to locate. You'll learn about that process and its many intricacies in the next chapter. So, what do you say? Let's publish an eBook!

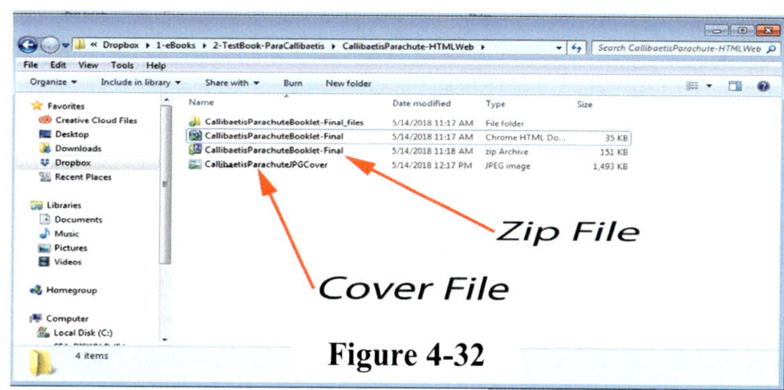

Figure 4-32

Chapter 4-G: Publishing A Kindle eBook

So here we are near the end of this eBook and at the exciting place we've worked so hard to attain. It's time to actually PUBLISH your hours of work and share it with a customer base just waiting for a chance to purchase it.

Sign in to your Amazon.com—Kindle account or set one up if you don't already have an account at https://kdp.amazon.com/en_US/. When setting up an account, you'll need your bank account and routing number information so Amazon and KDP know where to send your monthly royalty income. After setting up the account, use your password to access your author's page. You'll end up on an options page like the one in Figure 4-33. Be sure you are on the **Bookshelf** page and are ready to click the **Create a New Title** box called **+ Kindle eBook** circled. Take notice of the item below identified as **+ Paperback**. You won't need it now but if you ever decide to publish a print media book as outlined in the next chapter, it will be where you start the publishing process.

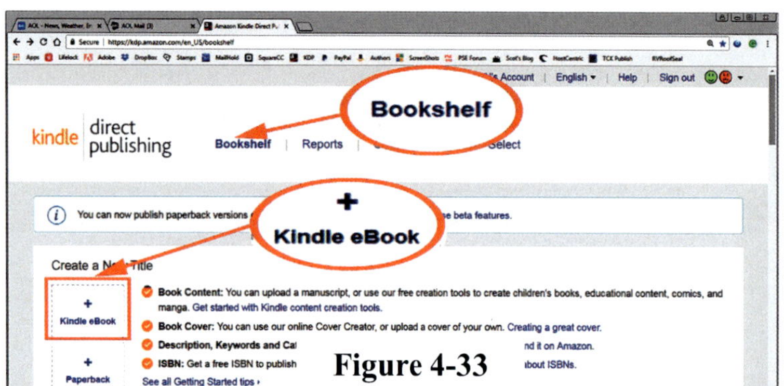

Figure 4-33

Before you click the **+ Kindle eBook** box, take a quick look at the items next to it. They include **Book Content**; **Book Cover**; **Description, Keywords and Categories; and ISBN**. Note you don't need an ISBN when publishing an eBook but will need one if you are publishing a print media book.

After clicking on the "box" the following screen comes up where we entered the book's **Title** and **Subtitle**. We do not have a Series or Edition Number so we left them blank and did not include them in Figure 4-34. We didn't see a need to take up the space but if YOUR book has those items, you'll find them located on this page directly below those you see in this illustration. They are self-explanatory once you see them.

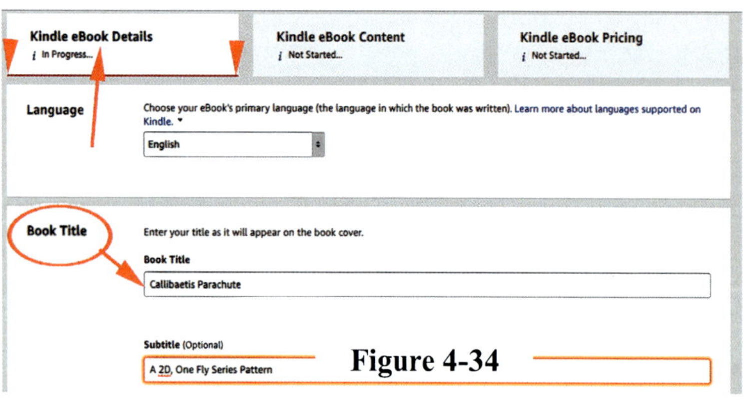

Figure 4-34

Next, comes the **Author** and **Contributor** sections followed by the book's **Description**. The Description is important because this is where KDP gives you 4000 charters to "entice" the public to purchase your book. As you can see in Figure 4-35 our description is "off-the-box" but there is an up & down bar available to allow viewing or editing the complete text. Also if you look close at the area below the box (lower right), we still have 3275 characters left for our description.

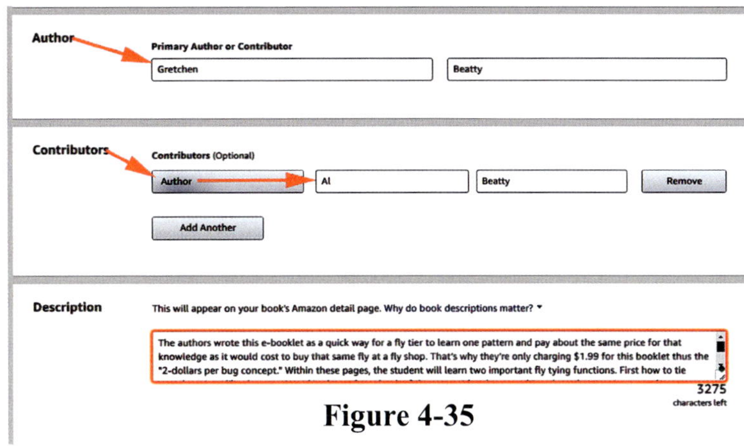

Figure 4-35

Next is **Publishing Rights (PR)**, **Keywords**, and **Categories** (it's important to check a PR option, we selected that WE own the rights to the book). The other two items will help potential customers find your eBook using the Amazon search engine. You may choose two Categories and we selected **Nonfiction – Crafts & Hobbies** and **Nonfiction – Nature, Environment**. See Figure 4-36.

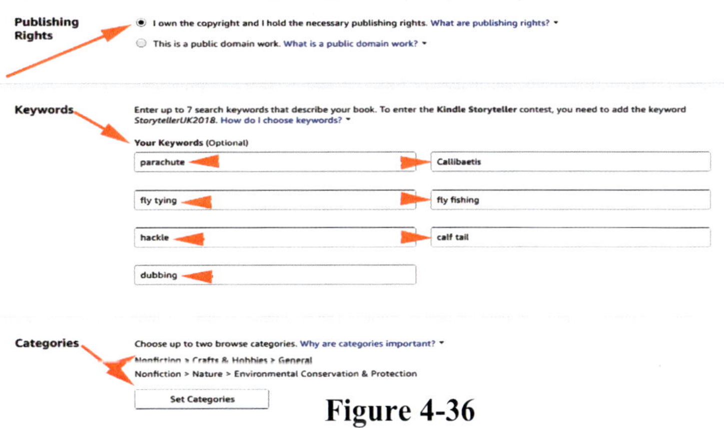

Figure 4-36

We try to write our eBooks so just about any age group can understand them so we did not check the age or grade section. We DID check the "button" labeled **I am ready to release my book now** as indicated here in Figure 4-37. Now click the **Save and Continue** box; see the red arrow pointing at the bottom right, orange box.

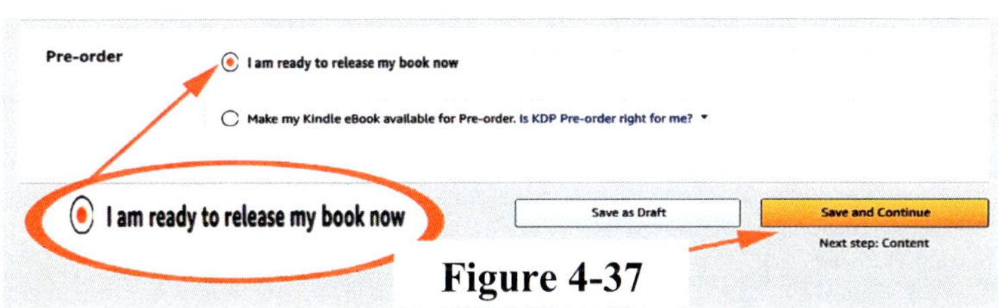

Figure 4-37

Now we are getting to the fun stuff but first (on the next page) we need to select **Digital Right Management (DRM).** Hover over the hyperlink and read about your options to help make the best decision. We selected **Yes**. The next two items are uploading our

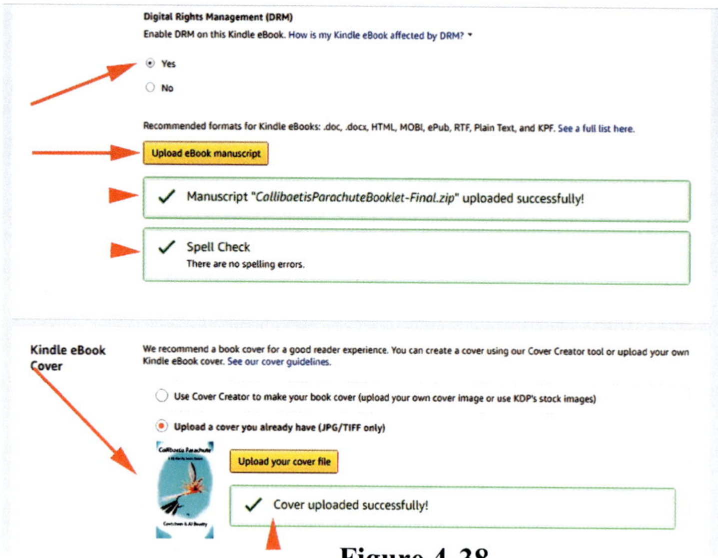

Figure 4-38

manuscript ZIP file And the cover JPG. See Figure 4-38.

Notice we had a successful upload of our manuscript AND cover. Also, the KDP **Spell Check** did not find any errors. Good news! We'll skip the **Kindle Preview** and go straight to the bottom of the page where we'll click the **Save and Continue** button so we can progress to the pricing page.

The first options on the pricing page are **KDP Select** and **Territories**. We always choose **KDP Select** and ALL of the **Territories** which means we are offering our book for sale in 18 countries including the USA. See Figure 4-39. The first time you publish with KDP, you'll have to select the Territories you'd like to sell in. We picked them all so we didn't miss any potential customers.

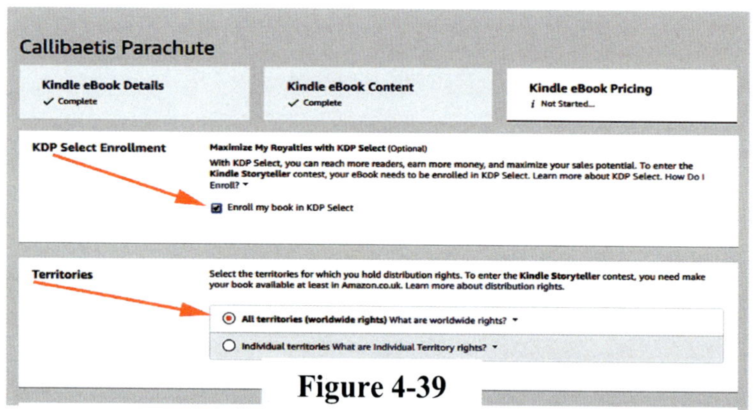

Figure 4-39

Now we are near the end where we pick **Royalty and Pricing**. You have two royalty options, 35% or 70%. The price you charge determines which one of the two percentages KDP allows you to select. The percentage number is the amount of the total price **YOU** get for each sale.

First, we'll discuss an abbreviated guideline to the 35% royalty option. The book must be priced somewhere between $.99 and $200.00 per download with no KDP download charges. That's funny! Of course, Kindle doesn't charge you for the download because you are giving them 65% of the sale price. You may wonder why anyone would choose this option but here's one example. A public domain "republish" MUST be in this category. Interesting! We didn't know we could republish public domain content. We'll have to check into that option at some point in the future! It could very well be another unforeseen publishing opportunity. We may even have to write a book on it.

The second and most popular option is 70% of the sale price for YOU and the rest for KDP. It also has some restrictions. The price must be between $2.99 and $9.99 per download BUT KDP also charges YOU a $.15 per MB (megabyte) "delivery cost" for each book sale (download). Now you can see why all through this book we've been talking about the importance of small, good quality files. If you have a large manuscript it's a balancing act between your income and what is charged to deliver your book to the customer.

With our Callibaetis Parachute book, we've already decided to charge $1.99 for it so our royalty is automatically set at 35% with zero download fees. As you can see our part of the sale price is $.70. That's not much but believe us, those little amounts DO add up! See Figure 4-40.

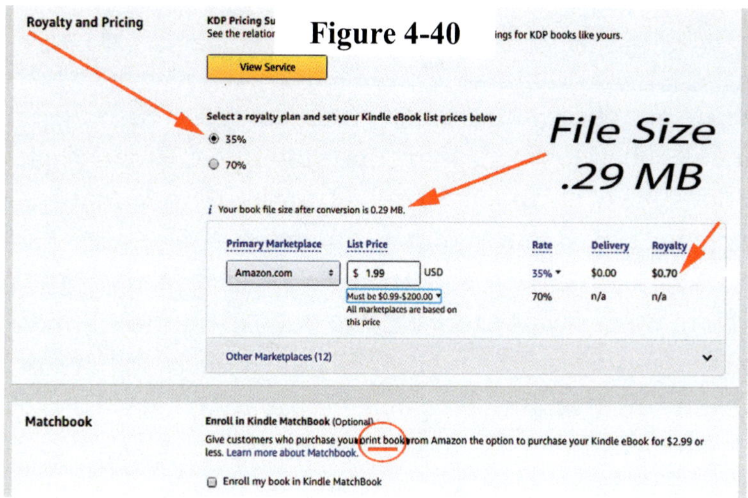

Figure 4-40

There's a couple of other items in the above Figure 4-40. They are **Matchbook** and **file size**. Matchbook is an option to select if you already have a print book on Amazon and want to add an identical eBook version. It's a way to offer a special deal to customers who have already bought your print paperback book.

The last interesting tidbit above is the file size of our finished sample *Callibaetis* eBook. It is less than 1 MB; in fact, it is exactly .29 MB. Of course, the sample book was quite small and only offered instruction for one fly pattern but it will give you an idea of the file size if you write a book with a dozen patterns. If everything is equal, a book with a dozen patterns following the methods and format we share with you here the file would be about 3.5 MB in size.

We are almost there! Just two items yet to complete. Click the box allowing **Book Lending** and THEN CLICK the **Publish Your Kindle Book** button. After clicking the button you'll get a message telling you KDP is processing your book. You'll get an email from them letting you know when the book goes live to the world. That can take up to 72 hours but we've seldom had one take more than a day or two at the most. See Figure 4-41 on the next page.

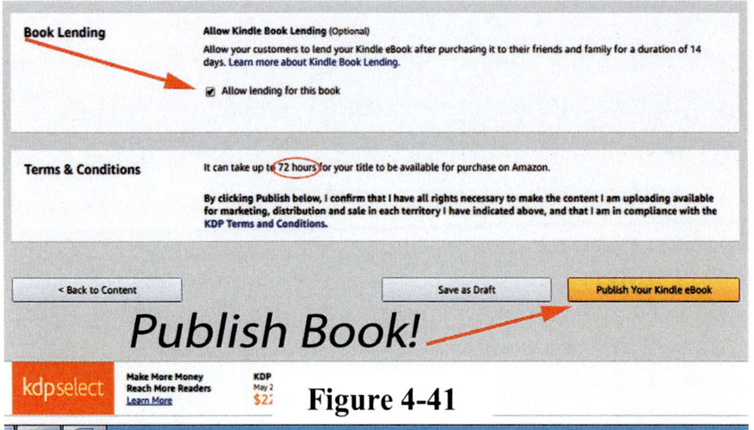

Figure 4-41

Before we leave this subchapter don't get the idea it's OK to skip the next and go straight to the new section on print media. Why? Because the next short section will be the **easiest publishing opportunity** you'll have in this whole book.

From our current position, we are about 4 mouse clicks away from a completed document. What do we mean by that statement, 4 mouse clicks? We currently have an eBook MSW document saved on our hard drive that we used to make the HTML file we uploaded to Kindle a couple of minutes ago.

While we are waiting for KDP to publish our new eBook let's put that MSW file to use making us a few more self-publishing dollars. What's best about the next section is it opens opportunities for publishing in BOTH electronic AND print media. I guess we could have called this next subchapter "The Crossover Media Chapter" but we'll leave the name like it is below. We'll let you decide how to best use its capabilities in your publishing plan.

Chapter 4-H: Publishing A Downloadable PDF

If you are not familiar with the term "PDF," here is the Wikipedia definition. "The Portable Document Format (PDF) is a file format developed by Adobe (the Photoshop company) in the 1990s to present documents, including text formatting and images, in a manner independent of application software, hardware, and operating systems. Based on the PostScript language, each PDF file encapsulates a complete description of a fixed-layout flat document, including the text, fonts, vector graphics, raster images and other information needed to display it. PDF was standardized as an open format in 2008, and no longer required any royalties for its implementation."

So what does all that verbiage really mean for the average person like us? It means anyone can create a document on a MAC or a PC using any program, save it to a PDF format, and anybody else on a PC or a MAC can read it whether they have the same program in which the document was created or not. All you need to read a PDF file is a free "reader APP" from Adobe, Foxit, or Windows often included with a new computer. Since its inception, the PDF format has become an important part of self publishing.

Now that we all know what a PDF file is, let's explore how we can use it for our self-publishing projects. Let's start with the eBook we just uploaded to Kindle Direct Publishing (KDP). We have the original MSW files we created for the uploaded document. We'll just change it into a PDF document we can use in a number of different ways. We'll start the PDF conversion by opening the file, expanding its view so we can see ALL of the document on one screen, and insert a blank page BEFORE the title page. See that view in Figure 4-42. We inserted the blank page by placing our curser ABOVE the text on the title page and inserting a "page break." The red arrow shows the **Insert > Page Break** tab.

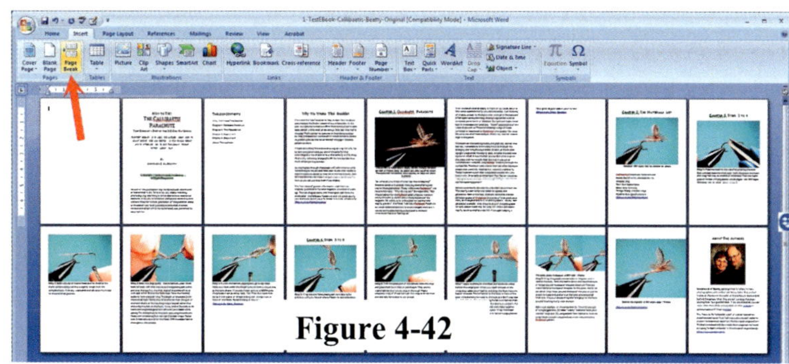

Figure 4-42

We have a total of 18 pages (including the blank page). Remember this is an eBook document with a 5" by 8" page size so before we convert this document to a PDF file we need to do a couple of things. First, we'll change the page size to 8.5" by 11" to fit a standard piece of paper and also insert the cover page file we uploaded with the book. Figure 4-43's red circle shows the page size tab and also that we need to PULL the corners of the cover OUT to fit the page. A larger page reduces the number of pages.

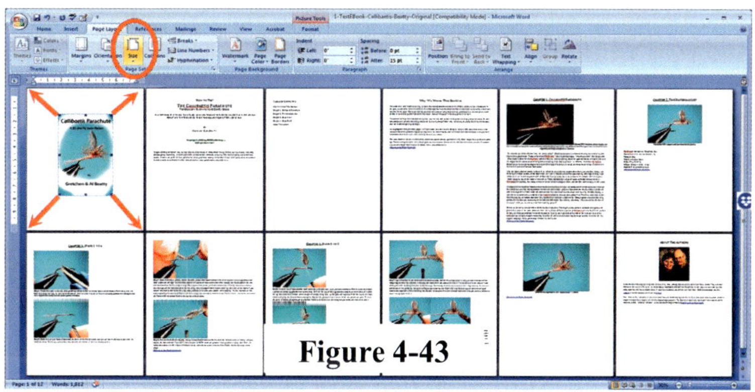

Figure 4-43

Once we click the **Save** button near the bottom of the screen capture (Figure 4-44) the file becomes a PDF and can be viewed on just about any computer as long as it has Adobe Acrobat Reader installed. All of the computers sold in the last 10 or so years has this program pre-installed as part of its line up of with-the-computer programs.

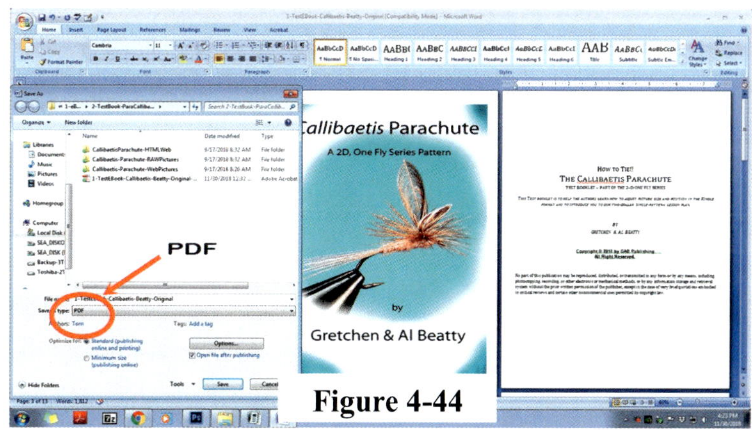

Figure 4-44

Now that the eBook manuscript has been saved as a PDF file, "What can we do with it?" This is where the fun starts and it doesn't stop with this chapter. We'll explain.

You have probably used one of the simplest forms of self-publishing when you e-mailed a newsletter, meeting minutes, and other documents to one or more recipients. The next step in this form of self-publishing is to convert the document to a PDF file so it can NOT be easily changed from its original form. We're not trying to tell you a PDF can't be changed because it can; it just takes programs and knowledge the average computer user may not have readily available.

The next step, and important to us, is the ability to post a PDF file on a website so interested people can visit the site and download it. It is much easier and less expensive to send a notification e-mail to club or home-owner association members that the meeting minutes or newsletter are available at the organization's website. Then the organization's people can download the file to read at their leisure.

Even better a PDF file is about one-third the size of the original file thus taking less time and expense to download. The two really important words in that last sentence are "expense" and "download." Why are they important? Because they introduce an added option for the self-publish author to offer information to customers other than via a Kindle eBook download.

What many self-publish authors may not realize is a PDF file of a book can be delivered to a customer using a dollars-for-book process similar to a Kindle download with one major difference; you keep ALL of the income from the sale. Earlier in this chapter you learned that as the author of a Kindle eBook you keep 65 percent of the sale price and Amazon gets 35 percent for marketing, etc. based on original sale price and they even charge you an additional delivery charge if the book is too large. Please understand, we are not running down Amazon. Their author's agreement is much more favorable than with other publishers but their service is not free and **they have distribution rights for a year**.

Here is another option. There are a number of companies who will "warehouse" your eBook PDF files and operate a shopping cart for you. Their prices are quite reasonable. For example we know a couple of authors who use www.e-junkie.com and www.sendowl.com. We've bought books from both and the PDF delivery was fast and professional. The price varies from $5.00 to $15.00 per month based on your needs.

One last way to sell your eBook is on eBay. The process is simple. List your book advising the delivery is electronic. Make the sale and as soon as PayPal notifies you the money has arrived, YOU e-mail the PDF to the customer. We do it often; it's very easy!

Chapter 5—Print Media

Over the years, we've been published in a number of different print media formats including in the mid-90s with our first book. Also, we've published many magazine and Internet articles before and since. During all those years we never received a fan letter from outside the USA. Why? We think it's probably because the publishers we worked with during that time distributed to the USA market only.

Early in 2016, we published our first eBook *How to Tie!! Wonder Wings*. Within a few short weeks, we received fan letters from Europe, the United Kingdom, and Japan. We were stunned! That had never happened during more than 20 years in the publishing industry! It really opened our eyes to the enormity of the Internet's global reach.

Kindle markets your books to 18 countries with more coming online on a regular basis. Enlarging your potential customer base to all those countries is mind-boggling. We've heard there are about 5 million fly tiers and/or fishers in the United States. Expanding those numbers to include 18 countries could open a customer base somewhere close to 75 million people. Wow! That's huge! If we sound excited about eBook publishing it's because we are! The results show up in our bank account every month as steady as clockwork.

As exciting as electronic publishing outlined in the previous chapters is don't think print media is dead. It's not; it's just changing. After publishing an eBook, it's not uncommon to learn some people don't use computers and will ask for a print copy of your eBook? It happened to us at the very first fly-tying function we attended where we shared information from the *Wonder Wings* eBook. Right after that event, we returned to our home office to "print" several copies of the eBook to send to customers who wanted it in that form.

Chapter 5-A: Printing At Home

There is not much work to print out an eBook. You need to change the page size to 8.5" by 11" to fit regular printer paper and add page numbers so you can update the Table of Contents (TOC). Oh! Also, you'll need to make a new cover because the eBook one is too small for printer-size paper. No big deal! Right? Wrong!

You'll soon find the cost of producing books using your home computer and printer to be easy but darned expensive. The cost comes from the little ink cartridges used in most home printers. We learned printing our *Wonder Wing* eBook was costing us about $15.00 in ink and paper and we were only charging $20.00 for it. What's worse we were not counting our time to print and spiral-bind the darned thing! We had to figure out some other way and we did!

The first cost saving came when we purchased an Epson ET-4550 bulk-tank printer from Costco. Using that printer reduced the ink cost from $35.00 per small cartridge to $10.00 per quart of ink for the four bulk tanks – the total cost was $40.00 for four bottles, one of each color. Do you have any idea how long a QUART of ink lasts? We don't know because we are still working on the original four quarts we bought for the printer two years ago– black, magenta, cyan, and yellow.

The second cost savings came from our photography. At the time we used (and still use) a black or colored background behind our fly photographs and step-by-step illustrations. When we changed the background color to white using Photoshop we realized an immediate 60% savings in cost per book due to the reduced ink expense; it takes a lot of ink to make those solid color backgrounds. The end result of our two cost-cutting measures brought our per-unit price down to much less than $10.00 each making home printing a very viable option for getting our ideas to the public.

Another item that makes the Epson ET-4550 printer an attractive option is the ink nozzles are Teflon and less likely to plug. When they do plug (and all inkjet printers will do so), they are easy to clean using the Epson software that came with the unit. Compared to the cost of an ink-cartridge printer (about $150.00), the ET-4550 is quite expensive (about $450.00) but that's because the manufacturer isn't subsidizing the printer cost with those expensive ink cartridges. Believe us. In the long run, you'll be better off with ANY bulk-tank printer if expense is a concern.

Figure 5-1

As you can see from our discussion in this chapter, getting into print media is really not too difficult. With a home computer and a printer, you can produce books from an MS Word (MSW) or PDF

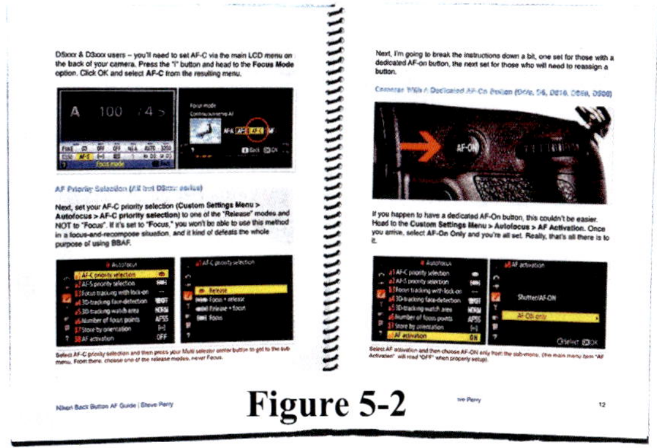

Figure 5-2

file. Al has been keeping the cost of his photography books down by buying downloadable PDF eBooks and printing them himself on a home printer.

For example Figure 5-1 (previous page) and Figure 5-2 are a book on the Nikon autofocus system by Steve Perry. It would have been expensive for a print copy but was free and only cost us the download bandwidth, the printer ink, and the paper. Some of his other eBooks have a nominal download fee like those discussed at the end of the last chapter but we think they are worth every penny. You will find them available on his website at https://backcountrygallery.com/. By the way, we think ALL of Steve Perry's photography books are great and NO we are not in business with him. We just like his no-nonsense, great-message photography books! Even though we are skilled fly tiers we still have a lot to learn about Photography and Steve Perry is one of our go-to sources.

Let's get back to printing at home. Our Epson printer has a feature allowing us to select printer settings to determine print quality. In fact, every home-office printer we've ever owned had those options in one form or another. On the Epson those setting are under File > Print > Properties > Quality then pick either Draft, Standard, Standard-Vivid, High, or More Settings (opens a slider adjustment page). After experimenting, we found using the Standard-Vivid setting produces the most pleasing-to-our-eye photograph on extra-white, printer paper. We use 24-pound, Xerox Vitality Premium Multipurpose Printer Paper available at Costco, Amazon, Wal Mart, etc. It's more expensive but heavy enough to stop "show-through" from one side of the page to the other. We think regular, 20-pound paper is better used when printed on one side only; the show-through from one side to the other using the lighter-weight sheet can be quite distracting to a reader. You'll have to decide which you think works best for you.

Making your book's cover: At this point, we'll assume you have printed your book and want to prepare a back and front cover for it. Of course, you can lay out your cover design with Microsoft Word (MSW) or Publisher (MSP), print it on the same paper as the inside pages, and assemble your finished product. The only problem is your finished book with a plain paper cover doesn't look very professional and starts to show wear-from-normal-use immediately. You've put a lot of work into your book and want it to look as good as possible. What should you do? For us, the answer did not come easy.

We tried several options starting by purchasing heavier-weight paper. The covers looked good for a time then really started to show the wear on the ink jet print. They just were not durable enough so we went back to the drawing board. By the way, in case you are thinking we should have tried a laser jet printer, we did! It did a good job but the refills were expensive. Oh! FYI! We also tried using a spray can of clear, glossy varnish from Ace Hardware; the darned stuff was really difficult to apply evenly. We ended up throwing away almost as many potential covers as we kept. We were back-to -the-drawing-board.

Our next option was to check professionally printed covers from a local print shop, Walgreens, and Costco. Some of those options ran as high as $30.00 per cover and for the most part, were just too expensive or weren't available in the size we needed.

Finally, we got the answer from a local high school student. Jason was a fly tier who was demonstrating his favorite patterns at our local fly-fishing club meeting. He was also selling a home-printed book of those patterns so we bought one to "help with his college fund." We really liked the cover on his book and asked how he produced it. Jason's answer gave us THE solution for our books and is revealed in the next paragraph.

The short answer is letter-size, hot-laminating pouches. We got the 9" x 11.5" size made from 5-millimeter thermal material which gave us a 1/8" trim area around our covers. We tested the same sized 3-millimeter pouches. They were OK but we think the book cover we get with the heavier pouch is a much better solution.

There are many options for you to consider regarding thermal laminating machines ranging in price from about $40.00 on up to $2,000.00. We settled for a 9.5" unit by Monroe (Figure 5-3) and seem to remember paying about $60.00 for it but understand we purchased it more than ten years ago. We did a quick Google search and didn't find the particular brand we purchased but there were many others available. Besides after you finish reading Chapter 5 you may very well want to try a different option.

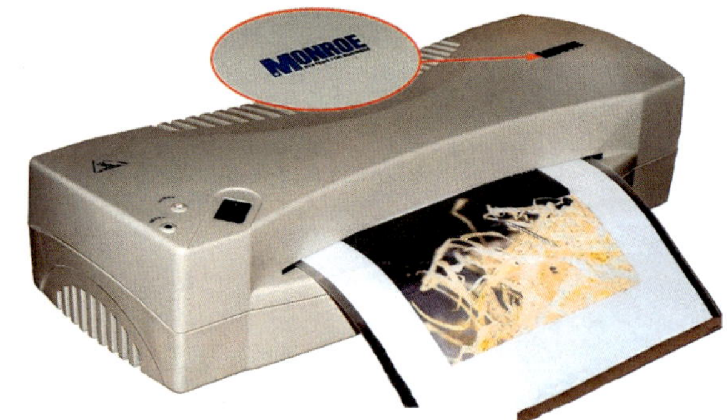

Figure 5-3

Binding the book: Once your manuscript with covers is printed, you'll need to decide what method you want to use to "put it together." Then are several options. You can use a heavy office stapler to bind them together along the spine OR you couple buy a 3-ring binder. We have used both and quite frankly did not find them an acceptable option after going to all the trouble to print the book! We tried two options. The first was plastic-comb bindings by Ibico. They required a proprietary Ibico punch to place the wholes with the proper spacing. The combs are really good for small books, class material, and reports. Once the page count exceeds 25 to 30 sheets of paper the combs have a tendency to allow pages to slip out of their control.

Figure 5-4

We think the best option is coil bindings because they do an excellent job of holding any size book as long as it's no more than about 250 pages (125 sheets of paper). Unfortunately, it's the more expensive option of those we've discussed. A punch can cost several thousand dollars but we got a smaller unit for about $100.00 several years ago. It will punch 10 to 15 pages at a time so a larger book will require several applications to prepare it for the spiral-coil binding. In Figure 5-4 a plastic-comb binding is on the left and the spiral-binding coil is on the right. If printing books in your home office and binding them yourselves sound like more of a hassle than you want, the next section could very well be your answer.

Chapter 5-B: Print on Demand Publishing (POD)

Remember on the previous page we promised "different options" you might want to try? This section introduces one of them and you can see by the title it's called "print on demand (POD)."

If you are not familiar with the POD concept it is fairly straight forward. Instead of having a publishing company do the book's layout then design the front and back covers, YOU do it all yourself. After writing your book, laying it out, and designing the cover YOU upload it to a POD company to warehouse the book's files until a copy is needed. When you or a customer places an order instead of a shipping clerk walking over to a shelf and pulling a book to ship, a computer accesses the book's file, prints it, and ships it to the customer. There is NO need to manage inventory because the book is not a book until someone orders it. That is when the book it's printed and shipped.

So, how do you get started with the POD process? First, you decide which POD company you want to work with then visit their website to find and download a list of their manuscript and cover publication specifications.

When you do a Google search using a "print on demand" (POD) query you'll find many companies offering that service. They include but are not limited to Blurb, Create Space, Amazon, and many, many more.

We've checked them all and for us nothing beats Amazon. Why? It's because they publish our eBooks, handle the "shopping cart," do the marketing, do the printing for our paperback books, and the list goes on. In other words, the other companies are good but for us Amazon does it all and they do so for a nominal download charge (eBooks) or for a minimal printing-shipping charge (POD books). The best argument in their favor is that their upfront publishing cost is free to you. That's right! Zero! Zip! Notta!

When you work with a regular publishing business you sign a contract in which you receive a royalty varying from 8 to 10 percent of the retail value of the book except for those given for review and promotional purposes. Also, upon signing the contract you receive an advance on future royalties earned based on expected sales volume. Once the sales volume exceeds the prepaid royalty amount then additional royalties are paid periodically (usually quarterly) for the life of the book. IMPORTANT NOTE: If you decide to contract your book with a regular publishing business, be sure to have included in the contract that you get the rights to the book back at the end of a specified time period (8 to 10 years is normal) or at least have the "first right of refusal" to purchase the rights back from the publisher.

When you work in the POD world, you sign a contract with Amazon (or other POD company) for a predetermined timeframe (usually one year). At the end of that period you receive the rights to your book back should you want some other company to distribute it for you. Amazon prints and ships-or-downloads (eBooks only) then pay a 1-month-delayed royalty every month of about 35 percent of the sale's price. Understand the estimated royalty discussed in the last sentence varies based to the sale price of the book (a decision YOU make) with one caveat: Amazon requires you charge a price high enough for them to recover their book publishing costs.

Chapter 5-C: The Manuscript Template

We'll be using Microsoft Publisher 2007 to set up our template. If you are using a different version of Microsoft OR another program like Adobe's InDesign you'll need to "adjust" accordingly. Also, we'll not spend as much time and space with this template as we did setting up the MS Word template in Chapter 4 because most of the commands are the same. EXAMPLE: Control + P is "print" and Control + S is "save" in both programs. We suggest you go back to page 31 and review the use of the ¶ (pilcrow) if you are not already familiar with its use. It's an important formatting function "checker" for many MS Office documents.

We'll start by accessing the **Format Publication** drop-down menu on the left of the screen identified by the red circle and arrow in Figure 5-5. From there go to the fourth tab called Publication Options and select page size. In our case, the page is 8.5 x 11 inches.

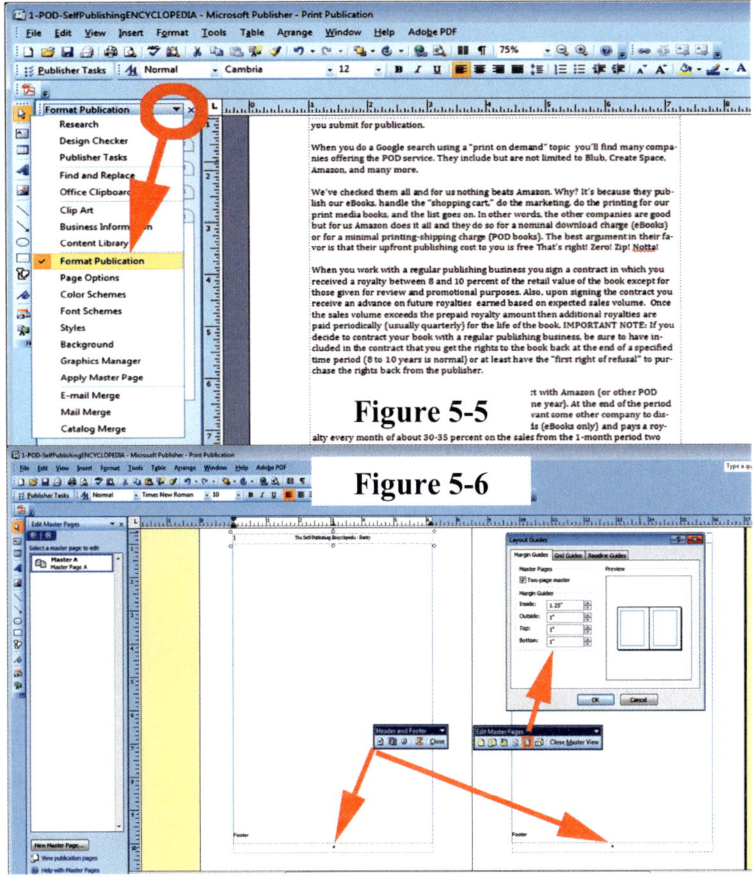

Figure 5-5

Figure 5-6

Next go to the top menu and select **View** then check **Two-Page Spread** then directly below that select **Master Page** (Control + M). After selecting the **Master Page,** go to **View** again and select **Headers & Footers.** Go to the left-hand page and click the header box. Type the name of your book in this box. You may justify the text as you see fit; we like to center it. Leave the right-hand-page header alone for now. Go to the left-hand footer, click on it, and select the number sign (#) to use as the placeholder for the page number. Repeat the process for the bottom footer on the right page (see the 2-red arrows). Next is the page margins (see Figure 5-6) set to 1 inch on ALL the OUT sides and 1.25 inches on the two IN sides to allow room for the bookbinding. This center area is called the book's "gutter." Your master page is complete and it's time to turn it into a manuscript template.

Refer to the menu in Figure 5-5. Near the bottom is a selection called **Apply Master Page**. Select it to access the option illustrated in Figure 5-7. In our illustration, we've elected to make a 48-page template (see the red arrow). If you need more or less pages, set the page count as you see fit. Add your page numbers via the top menu option **Insert > Page Numbers**.

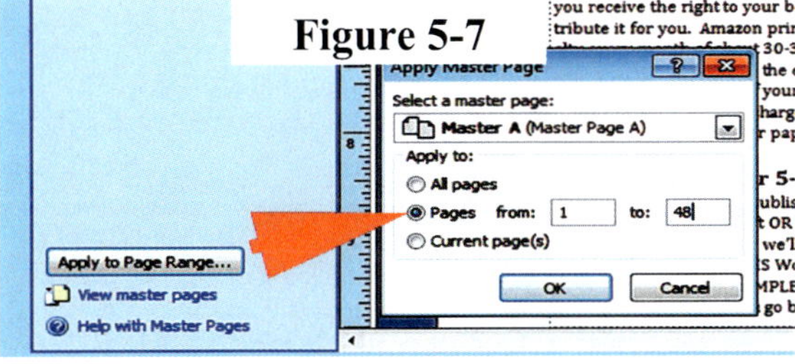

Figure 5-7

If you find our instruction difficult to follow you can access a pre-made template at our website (http://www.btsflyfishing.com) near the bottom of the home page. Use it with our compliments but don't forget to change the pertinent information like author, title, publisher, etc. so you get credit for your work rather than giving it to us. Just kidding!

Chapter 5-D: Editing Pictures For POD

Almost (but not all) of the information we shared regarding picture editing for an Amazon eBook goes out the window when we enter the POD world. For one thing, we referred to resolution for an eBook in pixels per inch (ppi) but POD is part of the print media world where we view our book on paper, not on an electronic screen. Therefore, in this chapter we refer to resolution as dots per inch (dpi).

The Kindle Print On Demand (KPOD) program "highly suggests" you use no picture with less than 200 dpi of resolution. If you accidentally place a low-resolution picture in your document, Kindle's "test equipment" will find it and "stop" the publishing process. We've never tried to override their stop warning, electing instead to make certain all of our pictures are 300 dpi in resolution.

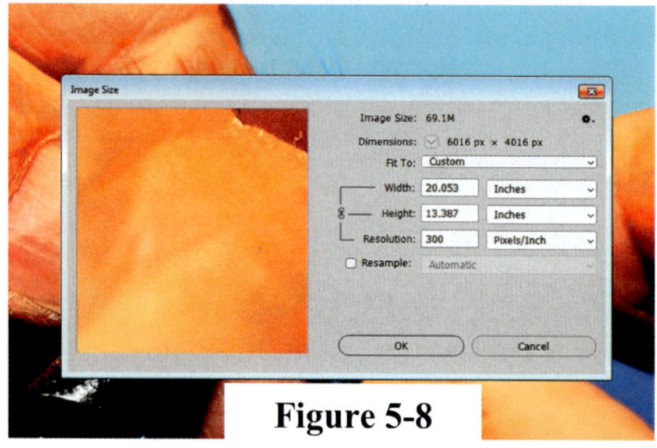

Figure 5-8

Read the next few words carefully! Sizing your picture for page fit in VERY important. What do we mean? Many of today's high-resolution cameras have sensors with 20 or more megapixels (MP). With that high of a resolution, the straight out of the camera picture will be 20" by 13" by 300ppi. Figure 5-8 is a file from our Nikon D750 with 24 MP sensor. Notice the image file size is almost 70 megabits (MB) before jpeg compression reduces it to about 25 MB (give or take). The picture will not fit on our 8.5- x 11-inch page. That's OK. After we use the **Insert** command to place the picture on the page, we'll just use our mouse to "drag" the picture corners INWARD until it fits our space. Problem solved. Right! Not hardly.

Even though we dragged the above picture INWARD from 20 inches to 4 inches, the on-screen-display picture is 4 inches BUT (you knew that was coming) the actual picture in the background is still 20 inches in size. That could eventually create a problem.

You see, KPOD doesn't allow a book file to exceed 450 MB and if our manuscript has 200 pictures that are 25 MB or more each we'll have a file size larger than allowed.

The best way to solve the problem is to reduce the size of the picture in Photoshop using the **Image Size** feature (Photoshop command = **Image > Image Size**) illustrated in Figure 5-8. In the case of the picture on the facing page, we changed the WIDTH from 20 inches to 4 inches. By changing that number the height is automatically reduced by the same proportion. After making sure the resolution box is 300 ppi we'll end up with a file size of about 1.5 MB. In so doing we can keep our file size down and still produce a good looking picture in our book.

There are two other reasons for keeping the picture file size down and they have nothing to do with the KPOD manuscript expectations. Instead, it is our personal computer equipment. When we start working with files larger than 150 to 200 MB it gets bogged down processing the data and will eventually crash. The other problem is our Internet connection, though fast, really "burns up" our data plan when transferring a large file.

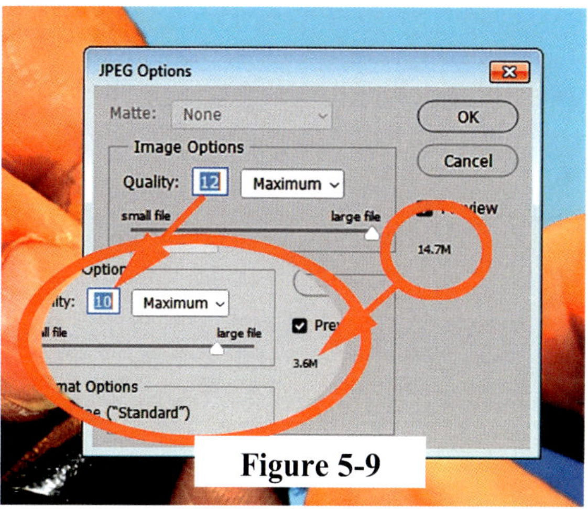

Figure 5-9

What we have done to "deal with" the problem is establish a few file-size guidelines. They are (1) all EDITED, camera-derived pictures must have a resolution of no less than 500 KB and no more than 3 MB and (2) all screen captures can not be less than 250 KB nor exceed 1 MB. On the rare occasion when we insert a picture that covers a full page (8.5 x 11 inches) we make sure to keep the file size to about 8 MB by adjusting the **Quality** setting when executing a **File > Save As** command. Usually, a quality adjustment from **12** down to **10** will do the job and doesn't seem to affect the picture quality; at least we can't see a difference. Best of all, that simple change substantially reduces the file size—see Figure 5-9 were the file was reduced from 14.7 MB to 3.6 MB.

Other Photoshop editing is just like post-processing for any digital image. We adjust Levels, Crop, Sharpen as needed, and save per the above suggestions regarding file size with one other tip. Be sure to save your pictures as jpeg's using Adobe RGB color space when possible.

We realize this section is quite short when compared to the lengthy discussion we put you through in the section on electronic publishing but quite frankly editing for print media is much easier. Why? Because your goal for print media is to produce a picture that is ONE size on a piece of paper. On the other hand editing for electronic media is more complex because you are producing a picture that looks good on a wide range of viewing screens from a cell phone to full-size computer monitor.

Figure 5-10

Before we leave this section on picture editing there is one other program we use to put a few final touches on a photograph. It might surprise you to learn that program is Microsoft Publisher—our layout program. Yes, it has a built-in "mini editing menu" that appears every time we import a picture or make a picture active by clicking on it. Figure 5-10 is a screen capture we made of the picture from page 62. The red circle shows the editing options available. Of the 14 options, we use exposure and contrast adjustments the most. **NOTE:** When viewing a 2-page spread, it is really handy to identify a picture that is a little too light or dark and adjust it so its appearance is the same as the other pictures visible to a reader. Figure 5-11 is an illustration of a picture that is too dark. If we click the highlighted icon (red arrow) a time or two the picture will get brighter. When it looks the same as the other photographs on the page we can then move to another page and verify that those pictures appear the same.

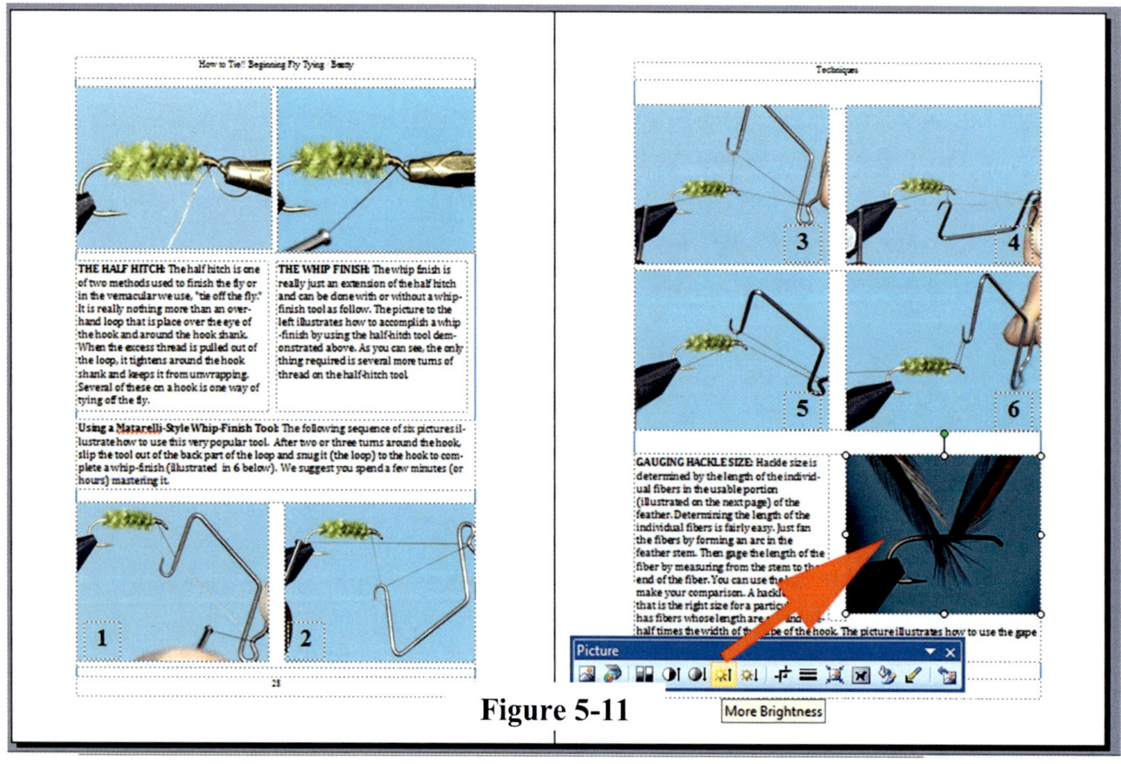

Figure 5-11

Chapter 5-E: Laying Out The Book

For the time being, let's set picture editing aside and focus on placing TEXT and PHOTOGRAPHS into our template. In other words after a lot of preparation we're going to actually start assembling our book.

We like to divide a book into several parts. They are the Title Page, Information & Copyright Pages, Table of Contents Page, the Book's Body Pages, and the Author's Page. The final part of a book is the back and front Covers that are completed as one file; we'll talk about them later in this chapter. For now, let's start with the Title Page.

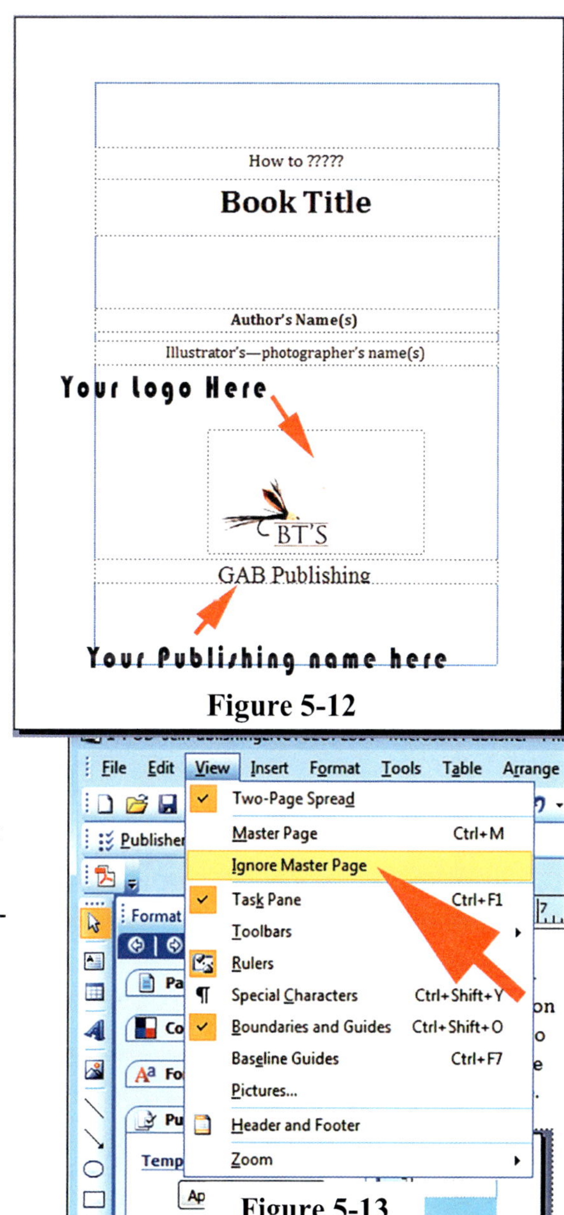

Figure 5-12

Figure 5-13

The Title Page should be on the first RIGHT facing page inside the cover. It's numbered PAGE 1 but the page number is "**hidden**." We'll discuss "**hiding**" the page number in a bit. If you set up your own template following our instruction and your "page spread" is two pages, then you'll need to **Insert** a page **BEFORE** the left-hand page. This is completed using the **Insert > Page** command from the top menu bar. Go to the newly inserted page and set it up as your Title Page. Figure 5-12 is a sample we use in our books. We have a free template for you to use at (www.btsflyfishing.com).

The next pages are the Information & Copyright Pages. Each book will have different information based on your preference. Take a look at pages 2—4 in **this** book to get an idea of what you may want to include in your book. Also, notice that there is no headers or footers on those pages but your template has them in place. To remove or hide them, go to the top menu and select **View > Ignore Master Page** (Figure 5-13). You'll need to execute that command for EACH of pages you want those items removed (hidden).

The Table of Contents (TOC) page is next and is the first page we do not turn off the headers and footers thus the page number will appear; we always make sure to place it on a right facing, odd-numbered page—page 5 in this book. The contents page should be fairly straight forward for any book; just type the page number where a chapter starts. Again, you may check page 5 in this book to see how we set our contents page up.

We do want to bring a handy MS Publisher tool to your attention. If you press **Control + F7** it will turn on formatting-only horizontal lines across the screen making it easier to "lineup" page numbers with the chapter titles when assembling your Table of Contents. Use it as you see fit.

If you'll remember when we set up our template we placed an automatic "header" on the left-hand page with the book's title in it but did not place one on the right. It's the reason you don't see a header on the TOC right-hand page. Except for the TOC page, we MANUALLY place a header on the top each right hand (odd-numbered) page as we progress through the book. We don't place a header on a chapter-start page but it's an optional choice. A sample is on the top of the next page

We placed that header by using the mouse to form a 5/8" by 6 1/4" text box at the top of the page in which we typed & centered the chapter number, chapter title, and our name. As we progress through the book, each time we "open" a new right-hand page we use the previous right-hand page to copy & paste the header. In so doing we only need to type a new header when we open a new chapter then just copy & paste it on the top of each new right-hand page.

Formatting the Document: Before we add text and pictures to our document, let's discuss how we'll format the book. Do you want one that is about the size of a regular library book (6" by 9") or do you want it to be larger like this book (8.5" by 11")? Before making your decision please understand that Amazon/Kindle charges **by the page**. If you elect to publish a smaller size, no problem, but you'll need more pages to do so unless you choose smaller font and spacing to fit everything into your expected page count. We'll talk about font and spacing in a minute but for now let's review a process called "trim."

If you use a ruler to measure this book you'll find it's less than our original 8.5" by 11" page size. In fact, it's about 1/8" smaller in width and length than the size selected in our MS Publisher program. That's because all of the paper pages don't align perfectly during the spine-binding process and are subsequently trimmed to smooth the edges. That's the reason's you want to keep your margins around the perimeter of the page back far enough so "the trim" does not cut off any of your text or pictures.

There is an exception to the loss-from-trim we discussed in the previous paragraph. That's when you want a color or photograph to extend **all of the way to the edge** of the page. This process is called "bleed."

The best way to get good color coverage on your page to the very edge is to extend the color or picture slightly past the page edge. Then when the machine trims the book you'll be certain to have "bleed" all the way to the edge(s) of any pages you design with that feature. Do we use bleed a lot? In books, we seldom do it but often have used it when laying out magazine pages. In some magazine situations, we'll have a color or photo cover BOTH open pages; this is called "full bleed."

OK, that's enough discussion about that subject. Now let's put text and pictures on our pages. We think it's important to size and space our text so it is easy to read and have thus selected **Cambria 12** as our base font, **1.1 spaces** between each line, and **double spaces** between the paragraphs. You may simply review these pages and decide if you think the extra space between the lines and paragraphs are worth the minimal page count increase. We'll use single spacing and indents for the next two paragraphs to help you decide which is easier to read.

Why Cambria rather than another font like Times New Roman? It's because we think it's easy to read and the name is located near the top of our selection menu in MS Publisher. Also, the text remains "clean" if we have to reduce its size below the base font Cambria—12.

It's important to use the same font size for different parts of a book. Chapter headings, first chapter letters, etc. should be the same so the book is graphically consistent from the first to the last page. If you wish you may employ the same **Cambria sizes** we use or select what looks good to you. We use the following font sizes:

NOTE: Below this point, the text has been returned to the original spacing

Body Text—12 (Bold only where needed)
Chapter Title—26 Bold
Chapter Subtitles—16 Bold
Material List-Titles—16 Bold
Material List-Components—12 Bold
Figure Box-Numbers—12 Bold
Photograph or Informational Captions—9 Bold

Now let's take a look at the picture sizes we like to use. If we want a picture to cover most of the page (within the margin boundaries) we size it to 6." That size is easy to see and fits well in the 6.25" space (see an example at the bottom of page 62). Also very important is the 6" file takes 10 percent less file space than if we increased it to fit our complete 6.25" space. That 10 percent savings may not sound like much but it counts up over the span of a book. Use the size you need to best illustrate your manuscript. We find the following sizes work well for the type of projects we publish:

Chapter Title-Page Pictures—4" x 3.2"
Project Illustrations—3" x 2.6"

Wow! After almost two pages we are finally ready to start assembling our document pages. We've made more than a few mistakes as we've ventured through the Kindle POD process and the one we'll share now is really IMPORTANT! It's how/when to put photographs and text into the manuscript. We'll use a fly-tying instructional step from our *Beginning Fly Tying book* to illustrate how this process works. We'll start by placing Figure 5-14. Under that figure are the steps to place each item in the manuscript. **Be sure** to **place them** in the **order** we present them under Figure 5-14.

Figure 5-14

The **first step** is to form a TEXT BOX in which to place our Photograph, Padding, and Text. That box is the large dotted-line square. The left corner is identified by the red circle (around the Text Box Icon) with the arrow pointing from it to the left corner of the box. The other 3 corners are identified by the other three arrows indicating the right-top, right-bottom, and left-bottom corners of the box.

The **second step** is to place the photograph in the upper left corner of the text box. It could also be placed in the right corner. If our pictures are not centered on the page, we like to place them on the OUT side of the page. Whether that positioning is to the left or right is determined by whether the page is a left or right facing page in the 2-page spread. It is VERY IMPORTANT to place the photograph using the **Insert > Picture > From File** command. Do not drag and drop it in place.

The **third step** is to click on the Text Box Icon and draw a tall, narrow TEXT BOX positioned to one side of the picture or the other so it will be between the photograph and the text. We like to make this box about 1/8" wide. Its purpose is to keep the text from running up against the picture. In other words, it provides "Padding" between the two elements. If the text runs up against the top or bottom of a picture you may also want to add Padding to maintain separation around it depending on your document layout.

The **fourth step** is to place the text. In this book, we typed it into the TEXT BOX but we'll also cut & paste from another document. Either works fine, it's your choice.

We use both methods and have even used a scanner to capture text from other documents. The main thing about text is to put it in after the picture and the padding. PLEASE take note and follow the placement steps as we outlined them. If you don't you'll soon discover that a picture, text, or both have disappeared. More than likely those missing items are still there and you'll have to click **Arrange > Order > Bring Forward or Send Back** to locate the disappearing items. When using that function it's easy to mess up other items on the same page. Take it from us and just follow the document assembly order we suggest to avoid "manuscript frustration!"

Formatting Tips: The text you are typing or pasting into a TEXT BOX doesn't always fit. Often there will be more words than you have space. We really hate to lose an idea while typing so rather than deal with "fitting the text" into a space, we'll just drag the TEXT BOX down so it is larger than will fit on the page. In so doing we can finish typing our idea before losing the concept in a dusty corner of our mind's filing cabinet. Once we've committed the idea to text then we'll cut and past the overflow text to the top of the next page. Yes, we know MS Publisher will automatically flow the text to another page. We don't know why but using this feature causes us to lose text. Figure 5-15 is a sample of how we built the previous page using our drag-down-and-continue-typing method. The highlighted text is the overrun that we had to move to the top of the next page. Once we've cut and pasted the overrun text to the top of the next page we'll use our mouse to drag the TEXT BOX back up to its original position (see the red circle above) so that "page 66" is the last thing on the page, NOT our overrun.

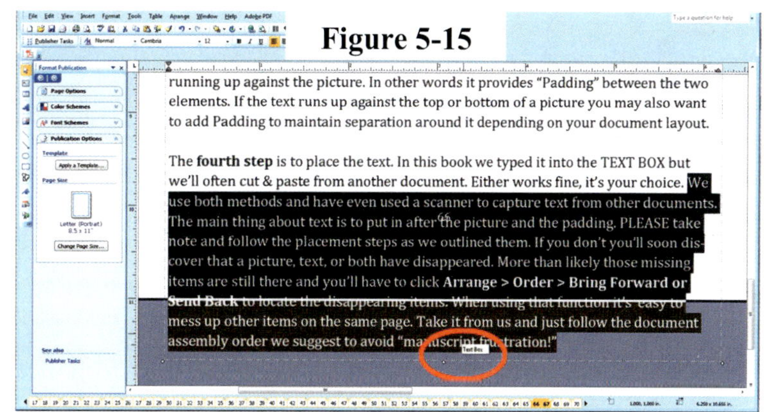

Figure 5-15

Another important consideration is the overrun warning icon illustrated in Figure 5-16. It is the "A" followed by 3 dots. It indicates there is some type of overrun at the bottom of the active box. Drag the box down to verify you have not missed any extra text overrun. Often the warning seems to show nothing and you'll wonder why you're getting the icon but there is no evident overrun. Click at the bottom of the box and you'll find an unwanted space. Just use your backspace key to remove the extra space(s) and your warning will disappear. NOTE: An important editing function before publishing is to go through ALL of the pages, click on **every** TEXT BOX, and check for the overrun Icon.

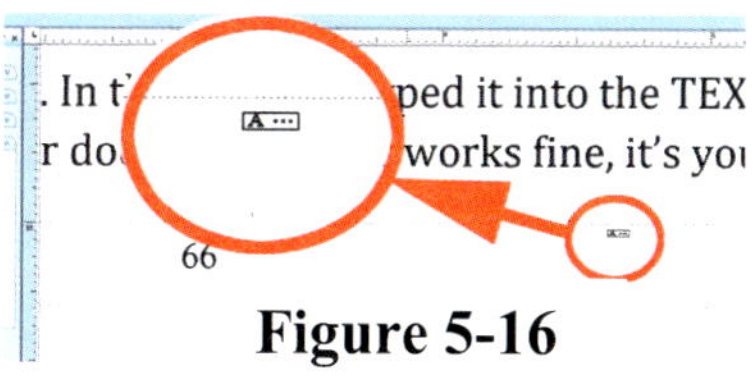

Figure 5-16

Placement of chapter and subchapter titles is another consideration. We like to place our main chapter titles 2" down on the page using centered, bold text. When we have space, we always start a chapter on the right-facing page then do not place a header on that page.

Notice the caveat in the last sentence about having space? When we are laying out a book that often has a chapter ending on a right-facing page the next page will be left-facing and blank. In this instant, we must make a choice. If it's a fairly short book, we'll use that blank page for "NOTES" and label it as such. When we have a larger book, rather than increase its cost (to us and our readers) with blank pages, we'll start our chapters on either a left- or right-facing page. In those cases, we'll put headers on ALL pages even if they are a chapter-start page.

The only reason we mention subchapter pages is this book has a lot of them. It's our first book in which we have used the concept. For the subchapters in this book, we double space between the last section and the new subchapter. We then increased the title font size, centered it, and made it bold type. There are a number of other options we could have used but tried this one as a test.

Before we leave this section on formatting your text we'll ask this question, "Did you notice in this section that we had "text flow" around the pictures?" If you weren't interested in electronic publishing and skipped Chapter 4 then you won't know what we are talking about. If you did read Chapter 4 though you'll remember we had to format our eBook text and pictures "inline." The reason we can use text flow around our pictures for print media is because we are actually **printing** the information onto pieces of paper. On the other hand, an eBook has adjustable text and pictures so the document can rearrange itself to fit on a wide range of screen sizes. We'll talk more about this later in Chapter 5-J on publishing your work twice should you wish to do so. It's important to remember when self-publishing. YOU—ARE—THE—PUBLISHER and can select any "look, medium, or style" you want for your book. You are the boss!

Chapter 5-F: The Book's Cover

We find it really interesting the smallest part of the book caused us the most grief. You'd be right if you guessed we are talking about the book's cover. In fact, it's not the whole cover, it's just one part of it. It's the spine. That skinny darned piece of publishing real estate drove us crazy and caused more rework than any other part of the print-on-demand (POD) books we've published. You see that little strip separating the front and back pages must be precisely measured based on page count. We have figured the problem out and will share our work-a-round solution in a few minutes.

Before we go any further we need to talk about cover options. You may not have a problem with the spine on your book if you use one of the templates Kindle Direct Publishing (KDP) provides. They are available as part of the KDP publishing process where you are prompted to make a decision whether to use one of their cover templates or upload a cover you've already prepared offline.

Quite frankly we've never used a KDP template but did spend a couple of hours exploring the options they offer. We didn't think their templates offered enough variety to illustrate to a potential customer why they would want to buy our book. No matter how we "adjusted" their templates the resulting cover would have been too similar to many others already in print. We thought their cover-from-templates were more appropriate for a novel rather than a how-to-do-it book like ours. You'll have to look them over and make the decision whether to use them or not.

We decided to employ the same programs used for this book to also assemble the three parts of a cover. We use MS Publisher (MSP) to set up the original template and follow up with Photoshop (PS) to design the front and back cover backgrounds. We also use PS's layers function to design the front cover however MSP works better for the back cover while using the background we designed in PS. It's not as complicated as it may sound so let's get into setting up the MSP cover template.

When we open MSP the first screen is the one where you select the page size you want to use. In our case we'll select "**create custom page size…**" in Figure 5-17 then enter the dimensions we'll need for our cover. The next information is IMPORTANT so don't skip over it even though it does have some boring mathematics involved; bare with us!

Those dimensions are 11.25" tall by 17.875" wide." The height measurement (11.25") will accommodate an 11" tall page PLUS 1/8" (.125") **trim** area on the top and the bottom for a total of 11.25" (11 + .125 + .125 for a total 11.25"). In case you missed it, we discussed **trim** in relation to book edges on page 64 in the section about formatting the document.

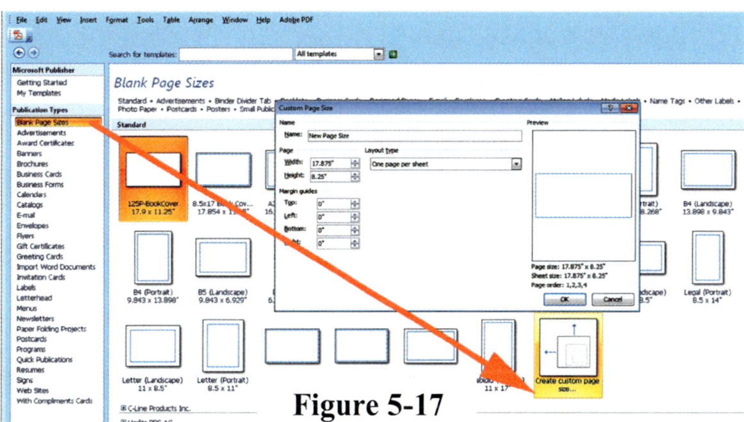

Figure 5-17

The width of the book is a bit more complicated because we are dealing with the book spine, the front and back pages, and the **trim** on the outer two edges. The spine is based on page count and for this book we'll assume when it's done we'll have about 150—160 pages (75—80 pieces of paper printed both sides). That means our spine will be about 5/8" (.625) wide. So let's add up our width dimensions. They are .25 + 8.5+ 8.5 + .625 for a total 17.875." You may be scratching your head wondering about the 1/4" (.25) in our group of numbers. Did you remember the **trim** on the outer two-page edges of .125 each? The spine measurement of 5/8" is a best-guess so we made it a little larger than needed but a good starting place. We'll show you how to deal with any extra width in the next paragraph. NOTE: Remember, the trimmed-off part of the book is called "bleed" in the publishing industry. Check page 64 if you missed it before.

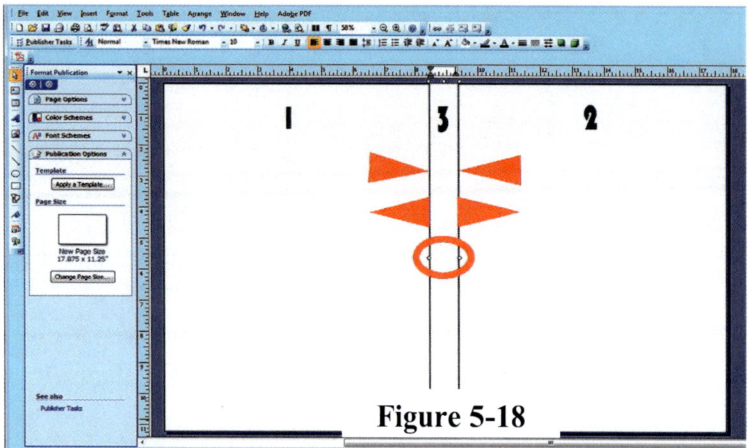

Figure 5-18

Figure 5-18 is the result of our work; the MSP template before we put any cover design data in it. We placed black lines around the three TEXT BOXES used to construct it so you could better see them in the illustration but for your own book you need not do so. Number 1 is the back cover, number 2 is the front cover, and number 3 is the spine. Notice the red circle around the adjustment anchors on box number 3 because it's the active TEXT BOX. Those anchors allow us to adjust the width of the spine based on the direction (red arrows) we pull them. If we pull them wider to accommodate more pages then we must move the front and back covers over an equal amount. Or we can adjust it as we'll explain in the next couple of paragraphs.

For now, let's set this template aside for a moment and use Photoshop (PS) to build a couple of items for the two covers—back and front. We'll open PS and select File > New then press enter to open a new file dialog box. On the right in Figure 5-19, we have the open box with our page dimensions selected—8.5 x 11 x 300ppi with a black background. Save this file as a jpeg called BackCover-Black.jpg.

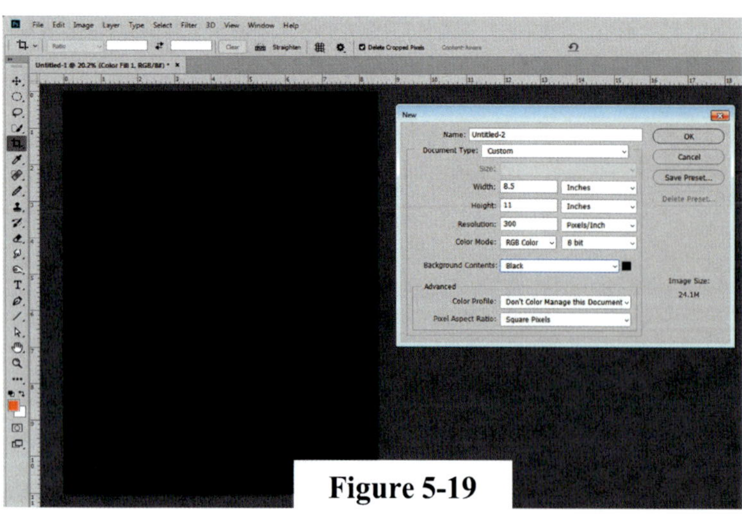
Figure 5-19

Figure 5-20

Now close everything and reopen the back cover file. Change its name to Front-Cover-Black.jpg and save it as well. We now have the background for the front cover of our book. We'll use our book *Hair Wing Flies* to illustrate what a front cover will look like after using PS layers to assemble pictures and text. Figure 5-20 is that finished cover. Save this file in PS as FrontCover-HairWing.jpg or an appropriate name to match your book. Notice we left plenty of space on ALL four sides for trim and other adjustments. You'll soon see what we mean by "other adjustments" when we layout the full cover in MSP starting in the next paragraph.

Now it's time to retrieve the MSP template we made in Figure 5-18 on the facing page and insert the two jpeg files we made in PS—the back (left) and front (right). We completed the front cover in PS so all we have to do is drag its corners out a very small amount so it fits the number 2 box in the template. The black file in the number 1 box doesn't have anything in it. It's just sitting there after we pulled the corners out to fit the box. It's time to put text in the description area and an author's picture below it with a short biography. Notice the yellow box in the lower right corner of the back cover. That's there to remind you to NOT put ANYTHING in that area. KDP needs that part of the back cover to insert the ISBN number during the publishing process.

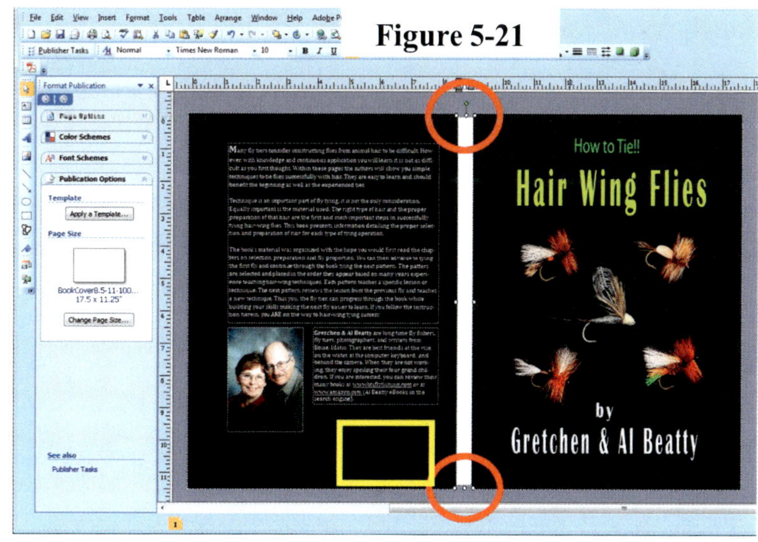

Figure 5-21

Notice the spine is still white and it's **shorter** than the two covers (see the red circles). That's so you can see that we actually dragged the two covers slightly OUTSIDE the template boundaries on their three outer sides. That little bit of extra is to be certain the **trim** doesn't cut off anything important on the cover. To finish the cover and hide the white spine, we activate the back cover and drag its right-hand edge to the center of the spine. Then we active the front cover and drag its left-hand edge to the center of the spine. Once that is done, we can save the cover as an MSP file until we review it during the editing process. If there are no problems found during editing, then we'll again save it as a PDF file for use during publishing. NOTE: If the KDP publishing program tells us the cover is not large enough we'll open the MSP file, pull back the front and back covers to expose the spine and adjust it in or out based on what the KDP program is telling us. After adjusting the spine, pull the left and right cover edges back over the spine to cover it up. After making that adjustment you'll again resave the file as a PDF, upload it and verify that KDP approves of our adjustment. More on this process in the publishing section of this chapter.

Comments Regarding the Cover: If you would rather not build your own template using our information, you can download one from the Kindle Direct Publishing (KDP) website at https://kdp.amazon.com/en_US/cover-templates. We've not had good luck using their templates but that's probably because they are designed for use with Adobe products while we use Adobe Photoshop for our pictures and Microsoft products for the rest. OR maybe we just didn't follow their instructions as we should have!

We've used 3 background designs for our covers—color fading to white edges, all one color, and dark fading to light in one corner. All look good to us but we've pretty much settled on the all-one-color option as our favorite. Figure 5-22 is a picture of those 3 designs for your reference. When we selected the color for the one on the right, we

Figure 5-22

thought a gradient design under the fading color looked good on our screen. When we got the "author's proof" you see in the photograph that underlying design didn't look nearly as good as we had hoped. Also the bright green "How to Tie!!" text color we selected looked really great on our computer screen but was next to invisible when we got the "proof" in the mail. We had to use a black felt-tip marker to outline that text just to take this picture for you to see the problem. By the way, notice the gray band across the middle of that book's cover. That band contains the words "Not for Resale" and is Kindle's method of identifying an author's-book proof.

Also, notice that the black spine we had used on the book in the middle has "slopped over" onto the front cover. We learned to fix that problem by dragging the front and back covers over the spine to cover it (outlined on the facing page). If you come up with a better system of keeping the covers and spine in alignment, please let us know via our website at http://www.btsflyfishing.com.

Chapter 5-G: Copy & Format Editing

Copy editing: We find it interesting. One of the most important parts of a publication is editing the content and this section will also be one of the shortest in the book? That should not indicate our lack of interest but to be honest, our text is either correct or it's not. Proper use of the English language is a goal we strive for and we manage to accomplish most of the time. That doesn't mean we're perfect but that said we are also not providing instruction on nuclear physics either. Our instructional tomes to date are about fly fishing, tying fishing flies, or cooking so we decided to forego hiring an expensive copy editor. We do the best we can following guidelines we've already outlined on page 40. If you find an egregious mistake you think must be corrected, please let us know via our website. One of the cool things about POD publishing is an author may correct their online book inventory (a PDF file on an Amazon Kindle server) at any time so future shipments are sent minus an identified error.

Format editing is a little more subjective and is often a matter of personal taste. We think it's important to maintain consistency in our formatting from the front to the back. If we place 1/8" padding around a photograph on page 6 then we expect to also have the same spacing around all other pictures in the book. We tried carefully going through each page and verifying ALL of the items we'll cover in the next few paragraphs. Quite frankly, we found we missed too much by trying to do it all in a single pass through the book. Instead, we go through the book several times looking for just a single item. We indicated above the first time through the book we are checking for padding around the pictures.

Next, we delve into three text related edits. The text size & style, line spacing, and text overruns. We can accomplish all three by clicking in a TEXT BOX and pressing Control + A to highlight all of the text in a box. That click presents highlighted text telling us several things. First, we look at the bottom of the TEXT BOX to verify a text overrun icon is not evident. Lack of that icon means the text fits the box and that's good. If you forgot what an overrun icon looks like go to Figure 5-16 on page 67 to refresh your memory.

The next things that highlighted text tells us is the text style is Cambria and the line spacing is 1.1sp outlined in Figure 5-23, a screen capture from the previous page 73. The box that indicates the text size is blank which tells us not all of the text is size 12. Upon closer inspection we find subchapter text that is size 16 font. It's the reason for the blank text-size-box—it doesn't know what to tell us based on the two sizes of font.

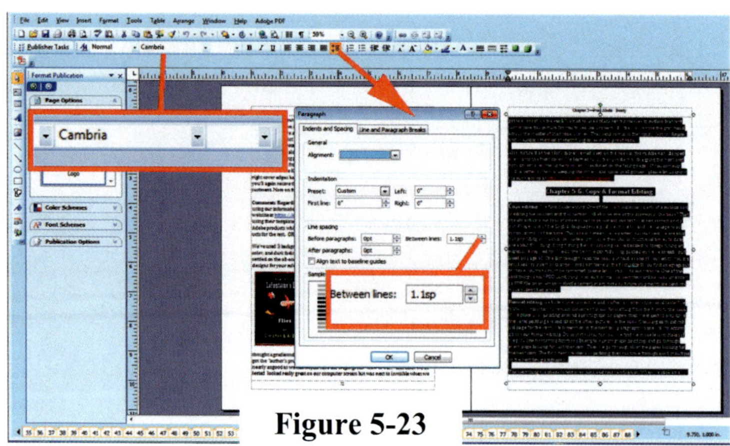

Figure 5-23

If we find the text **type** and **size boxes** both blank like we would on page 72 that means we have a problem to deal with OR a picture was highlighted when using the Control + A keyboard function. We'll have to check manually by mouse-drag highlighting the text below and above the picture to verify it a section at a time. This edit takes the longest; it gets easier from here.

Next, we'll do a 3-way check of the photographs. We'll start by making certain we are in a full 2-page view so we can see all of both facing pages. Check all of the pictures on both pages to verify they appear about the same regarding exposure. Figure 5-11 on the bottom of page 62 is a good example of how to identify a picture not matching its neighbors. Use the MS Publisher (MSP) mini photo-editing menu to adjust pictures as needed. Again, page 62 provides instructions for that procedure. While looking at the two-page spread, you also should verify all of the pictures have a "Figure #" and those numbers are sequential with that page and the rest of the book.

Our next pass through the book is to verify the text next to the pictures match what the picture illustrates. The way we set up our books we make sure to include the Figure # in the text to help with this verification. It also helps us keep our numbers sequential which is one of the editing functions we completed in the previous paragraph.

Our last formatting edit is to verify we manually placed a header on all of the right-facing pages except for the chapter-lead page. Quite frankly this is dependent on what you want to do with your book. We'll say it again, "You are the author, editor, and publisher of your book. Make it appear the way you want but be consistent with "the look."

Chapter 5-H: Publish Your Manuscript

Before we leave the book editing let us ask a question, "Did you remember to copy and format edit your cover. It's easy to forget; we did on one of our books and misspelled the title. We got it fixed but it could have been quite embarrassing.

Preparing your files: Before publishing, we set the manuscript and cover aside for a few days or a week then quickly go back through them one more time. Once that's done, our manuscript and cover must be resaved as PDF files to keep the Kindle program happy. To do so, select **File > Save As** then choose **PDF** from the drop-down menu as illustrated in Figure 5-24. The manuscript PDF conversion takes several minutes but saving the cover is much quicker.

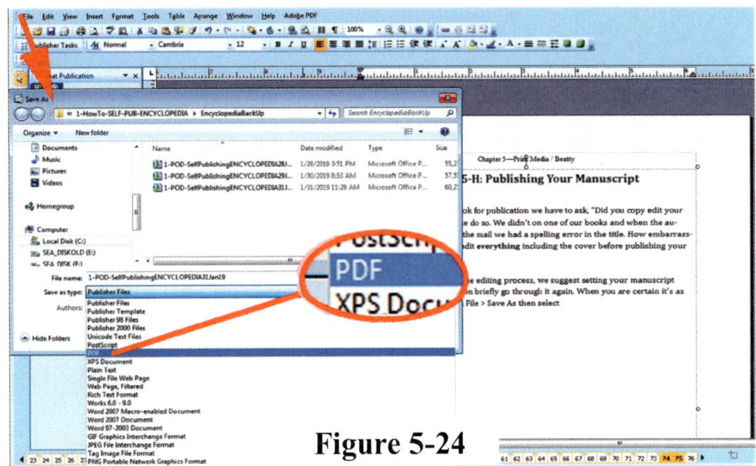

Figure 5-24

Publishing your work: At this point, we assume you have already set up your Amazon and Kindle accounts. That includes filling out the tax area information including things like your bank account number. All of that is a MUST to keep the Internal Revenue Service (IRS) happy and so Kindle can send your royalty payments each month.

Once that's done go to your author's page **Bookshelf** which should look something like Figure 5-25. Notice the red box in the illustration is around the "Paperback" "Create a New Title" selection rather than the "Kindle eBook" selection. As you can see from the dialog to the right, we'll be working on several parts of our book. For these illustrations, we chose our first book published as an eBook and as a paperback. When

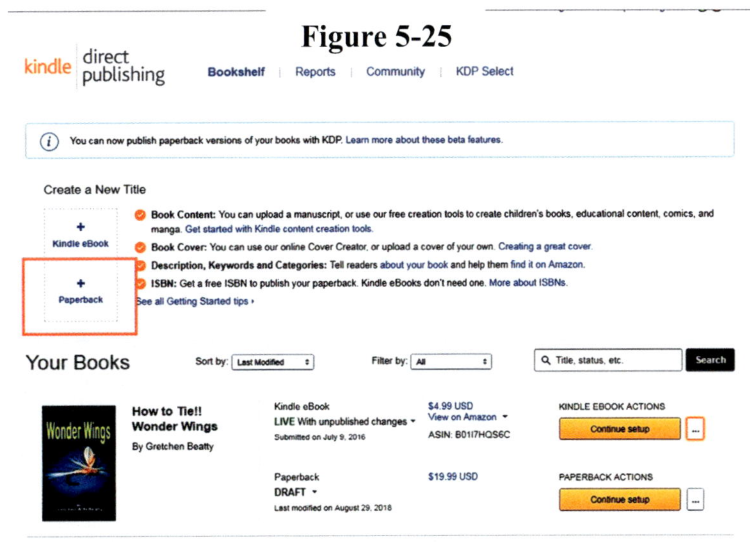

Figure 5-25

we click on the +Paperback hyperlink we'll be sent to the next page illustrated here in Figure 5-26.

Figure 5-26

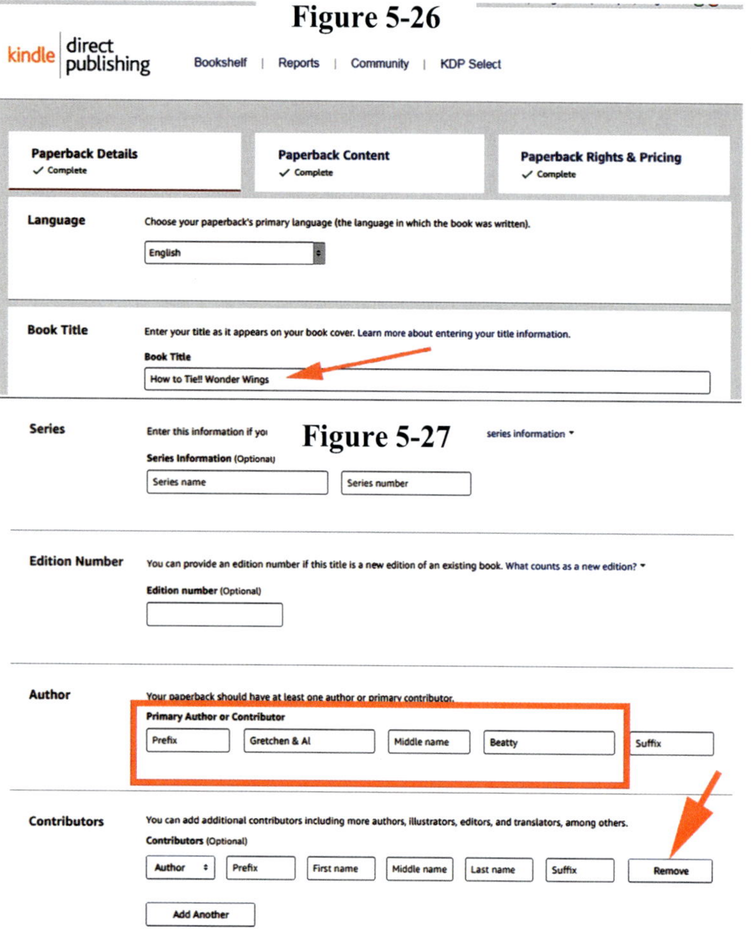

Figure 5-27

We had published this book previously as an eBook so some of the items were already filled out like the book's title here in Figure 5-26.

In figure 5-27 we added the author's names. We ran into a publishing problems because on the book's cover we identified the authors as "Gretchen & Al Beatty but when we filled in this section the first time we put Gretchen's name in the author's box and Al's name in the Contributor's area Nothing happened at that time but when we tried to upload the files and check Kindle's editing of our book, the system would freeze. After three frustrating days, we finally figured out the problem and changed the "author's names as you now see them inside the red box. Be sure you are consistent. Do not put a middle initial in one place and not in another. Lesson learned!

Figure 5-28

Description — This will appear on your book's ... atter?

This is a first in a series of fly-tying books that teaches the reader how to tie a single discipline and do it well. In it the reader will learn how to tie Wonder Wing flies from soup to nuts so to speak. You will learn how to "manufacture" the perfect set of wings in much less time than it takes to "locate" them by searching through a bunch of feathers or a neck. Have you noticed

3002 characters left

Publishing Rights

- I own the copyright and I hold necessary publishing rights. What are publishing rights?
- This is a public domain work What is a public domain work?

Keywords — Choose up to 7 keywords that describe your book. To enter the Kindle Storyteller contest, you need to add the keyword StorytellerUK2018. How do I choose keywords?

Your Keywords (Optional)

wonder wings	fly tying
pheasant feathers	divided wings
wings	Trude wings
hackle wings	

Figure 5-28 is self-explanatory. Here is where you entice a potential customer into buying your book using a multiple word description and search engine keywords and phrases that will position it toward the top of a Google online query. It's an important part of your marketing with complete books written on the subject. In fact, we are currently researching that topic ourselves. For now, this is a book on self-publishing with only a few marketing ideas in a future chapter on using YouTube videos to sell your book.

While on the marketing subject, Figure 5-29 demonstrates another important topic. That is selecting the proper Amazon search categories again so a customer can find your book on their website.

Your paperback book must have an International Standard Book Number (ISBN). You have a choice illustrated in Figure 5-30. You can get a free one from Kindle or buy one from Bowker (the official ISBN agency for the USA). If you buy it, the cost is around $250.00. The choice is yours.

Figure 5-31 highlights print and cover options. Each topic has a hyperlink to an explanation of options. It is self-explanatory. You can see which option we selected for the *Wonder Wings* book. It's also the selection used on our other POD paperbacks.

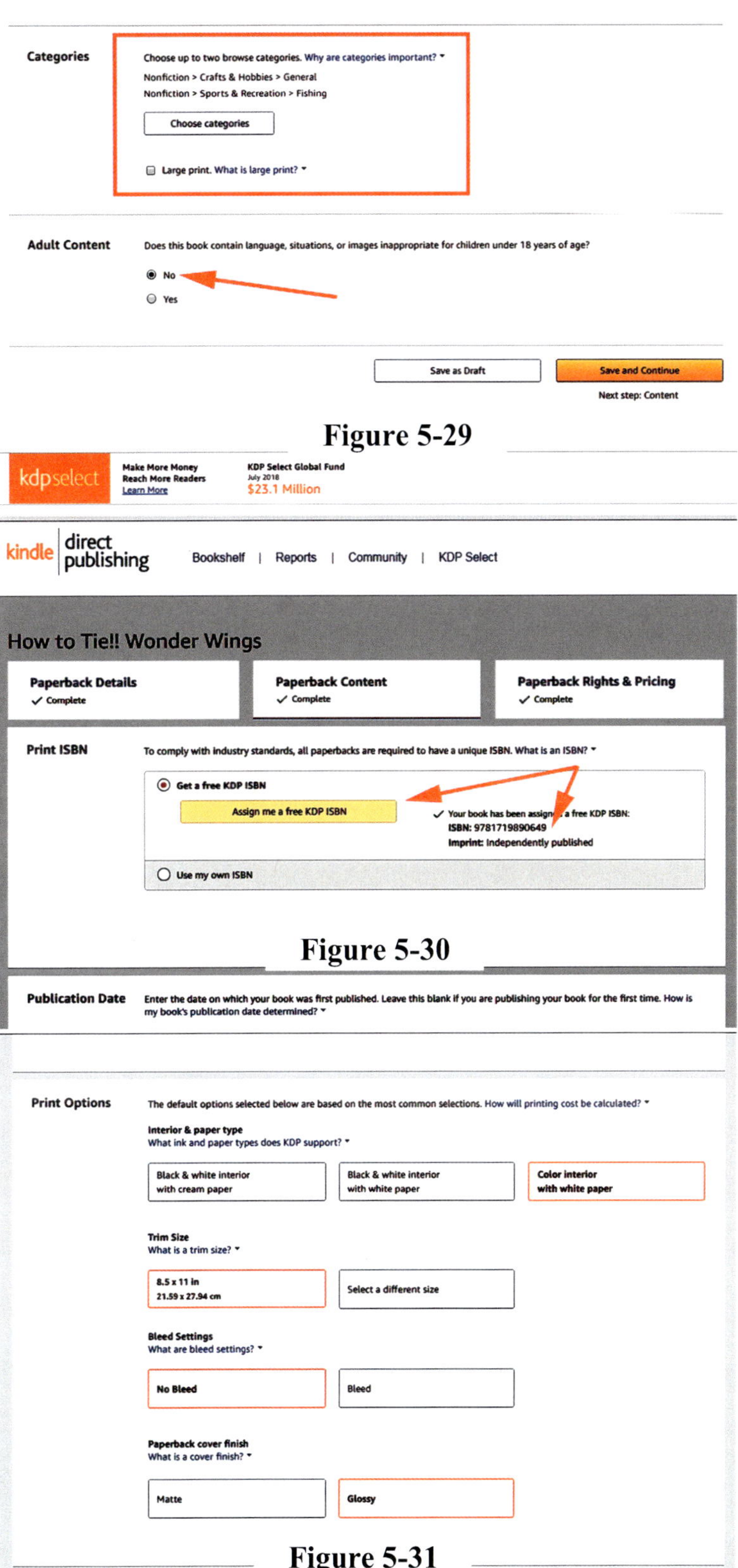

Figure 5-29

Figure 5-30

Figure 5-31

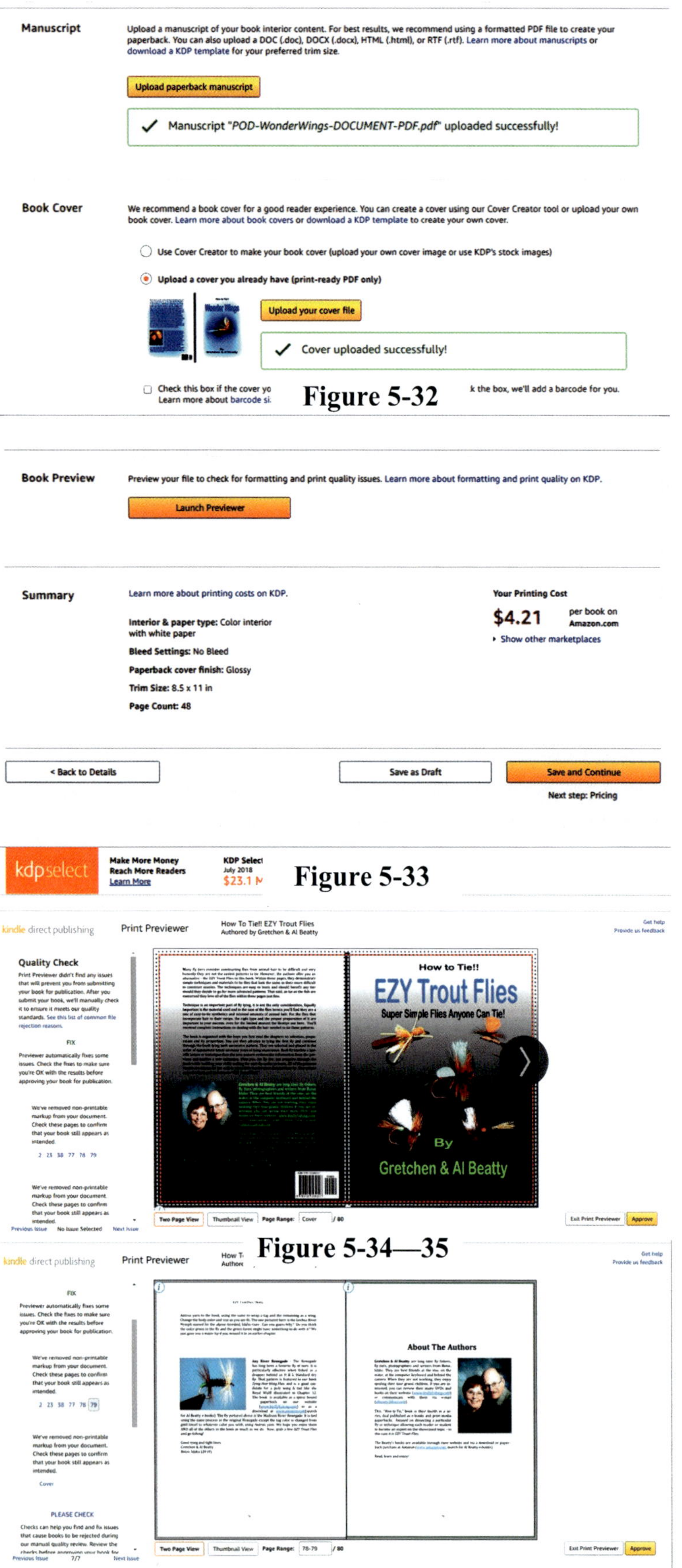

Figure 5-32

Figure 5-33

Figure 5-34—35

In Figure 5-32 we have uploaded the manuscript PDF file and the cover PDF file. In fact, you can see both uploaded without incident.

After uploading the files Figure 5-33 shows what the book will cost and we are presented with the option of reviewing the book before continuing.

We made a mistake while gathering screen captures and the 2-review pages are of another book we published rather the *Wonder Wing* example we've used up to now.

Figures 5-34 & 35 are what those review pages look like. In 34 (top) we see the cover with a red box around it. That line is where the Kindle press will trim the book. Be sure nothing will be cut off while trimming the "bleed." The white arrow in the black circle is how to step through the book.

Figure 5-35 is an example of a mistake Kindle found for us. Not all of the text next to the picture on the left page reached the padding. We fixed it!

Figure 5-36 is the marketing territories we've selected—worldwide. The next item is pricing and we've selected $19.99 as our book price. To the right is the book cost to us (the authors) and the royalty paid on ONLY the BOOKS Kindle sells for us. The books we buy for resale are not eligible for a royalty. We always check the box for Expanded Distribution should Amazon sell our book to stores like Barnes & Noble, etc.

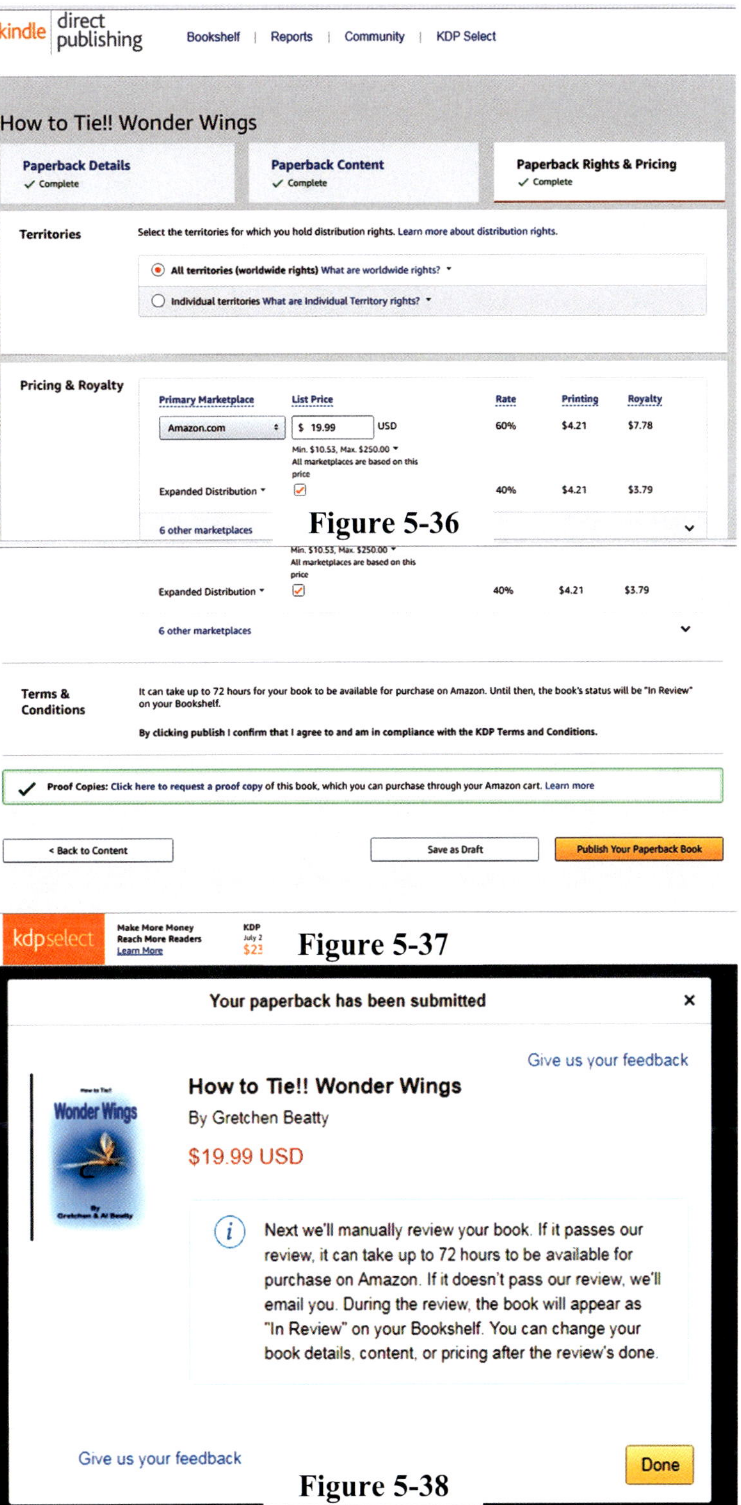

Figure 5-36

Figure 5-37

Figure 5-38

Do NOT click the "Publish Your Paperback Book" icon yet, we have a few things to do first. The next item is to order author's proofs (green box) in Figure 5-37 which brings up the message below in Figure 5-38. It tells us to wait while Kindle checks our book. We'll receive an e-mail when we can finish our author's proof order. By the way, we can't purchase more than 5 author's proofs but seldom purchase more than two so the two of us each have a "proof" to check over. Their message in Figure 5-38 indicates it could take 72 hours to get approval to complete your author's proof order but we've only had it take that long once in 8-publishing sessions with Kindle. Usually, we have confirmation back from them the next day. This is IMPORTANT: Click the "Save as Draft" icon for now to put your publishing session on hold. We'll pick it up later after our author's proof arrives in the mail and we've reviewed it.

Once we've reviewed the author's proof we'll need to make any corrections required to the ORIGINAL MS Publisher file then again save it as a PDF. If the cover is OK, leave the file as is OR make changes if needed then re-save it as a PDF. Now go back to Figure 5-32 at the top of page 78 and repeat the steps starting with the upload of any files you had to change. Once you are sure your book is good-to-go, click the "Publish Your Paperback Book" icon highlighted in Figure 5-37.

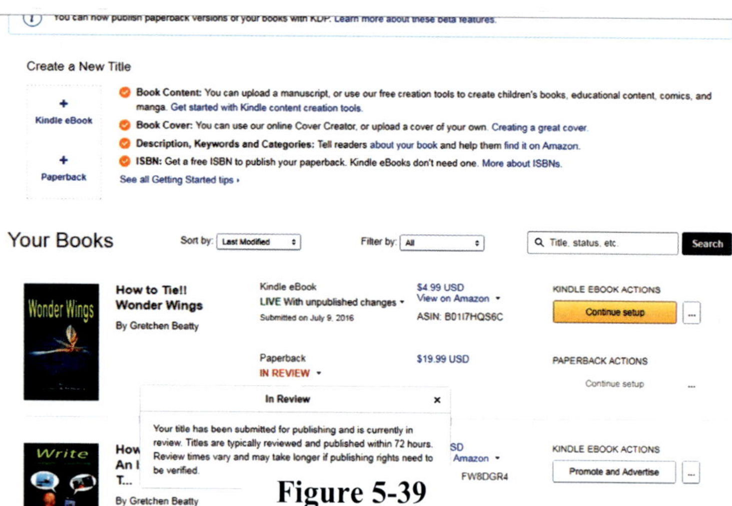

Figure 5-39

While all of the above is going on you'll see the words "In Review" in red letters (Figure 5-39) next to your book's title on your Bookshelf page. Once you receive your e-mail notifying the book is LIVE on Amazon you may order any "author's copies" you want to sell to family, friends, customers, etc.

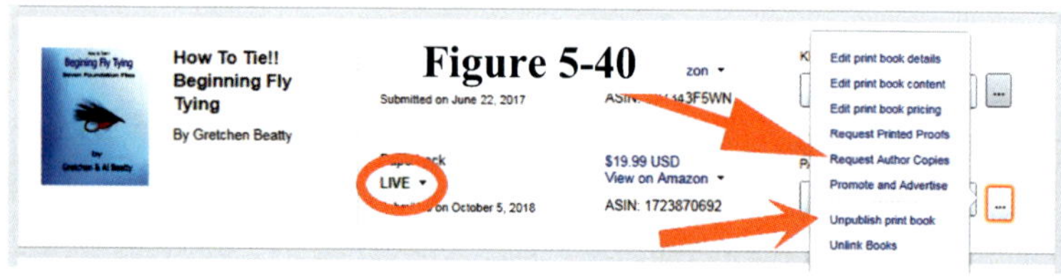

Figure 5-40

To purchase author's copies, go to your Bookshelf, find the book you want to order, and click the little 3-dot icon to the far right of the title. Clicking that icon brings up an 8-item menu. The top red arrow pointing from the figure number is the selection you make to complete your order.

Remember earlier in this chapter in the section on covers we discussed a spelling error on the cover of one of our books. We didn't discover it until after publishing the book. It was "live" on Amazon indicated by the red circle in Figure 5-40. We learned the problem wasn't the end of the world but it did have us sweating bullets for a while. We're now glad it happened because we learned how to fix errors in a book or on its cover. The second to the last item on the same 3-dot icon highlighted in Figure 5-40 is where you "Unpublish print book." Click that icon, fix what needs to be repaired, and again upload the file(s) that had to be corrected. We had to again go through the publishing process on page 78 like before but soon we had a corrected book for sale.

Chapter 5-I: Multiple Publishing Platforms

Let's discuss publishing on more than one platform. When we started "publishing" our first paperback at the beginning of Chapter 5-H, we indicated the eBook had already been published. We also were able to demonstrate much of the online publishing form was already filled out from our previous eBook entries. So it's obvious we can easily publish our work as an eBook AND a paperback book. There is another method to publish our work and that's via an audiobook. We'll delve into that option more in the next chapter but for now we'll talk about electronic and print publishing.

You may want to follow in our footsteps and publish your book first as an eBook and then as a paperback via print media. One reason to do so is an eBook is quicker to put together and publish. Why? There is a lot of editing and formatting for a print-media book not needed with an eBook.

You are probably wondering, "Why not just take the eBook manuscript and publish it as a paperback?" There are two reasons that doesn't work. We've already discussed the different resolution requirements in pictures between electronic and print-media documented in both Chapters 4 & 5. We also need to compare "word wrap text" and "inline text." If you would like a quick refresher on those two items go to page 36 and view Figures 16 and 16A.

In line text is used so the Kindle eBook program can easily adjust picture and text sizes based on the dimensions of the viewing screen. On the other hand, the printed page is static. Once it's formatted on a piece of paper it stays the same size and arrangement.

You could format your print book so it's text is inline but your book would be many pages longer than it needs to be. Look at all of the lost print space in Figure 16A on page 36. Every picture would have that same loss. The extra pages would drive up the cost of your book.

Another Possibility: When we wrote Chapter 4 there was no real solution to the inline text dilemma but true to its word KDP did come up with a solution of sorts but it does have a major problem. We'll discuss the problem in a few sentences but first let's talk about their solution.

KDP rewrote their computer program so a self-publishing author could upload the PDF file of a print-media book after reducing the picture file size to meet their parameters. The easiest way to do so is by editing and replacing the picture's jpeg file (Chapter 4-C) in the MS Publisher manuscript then save that lower resolution version as a PDF.

We were really excited when we learned of their publishing "improvement." Instead of taking several days or weeks to convert an eBook to print, we could just change the pictures and republish. It sounded great in theory but in reality it had a problem. When we tested the program it did, in fact, do everything they stated EXCEPT the page resizing did not ADJUST to fit the viewing screen. In the newly uploaded PDF file when we viewed a page with pictures (Example page 80), it looked OK but on a cell phone the picture was about a half-of-an-inch wide and the text was so small we couldn't read it. No big deal, we'd just use our fingers to "zoom" on the Smartphone screen. The screen enlarged so we could easily see the picture and the text but both would also disappear off the right side of the screen. We had to keep scrolling it back and forth to read a page. What a pain!

There was no text and image resizing or adjusting to page size. We were really disappointed. We recommend you reformat your manuscript based on the methods detailed in Chapter 4. You can do the quick and dirty method (PDF upload) but we think your readers will not be happy. It's your choice.

Chapter 5-H: Spines & Re-Binding

In some instances, you may want to offer your customers a different reading experience than what a Print On Demand (POD) KDP book offers. What do we mean by that? Let's talk about the book's spine.

A Kindle book arrives in your reader's mailbox with a glued spine just like all other paperback books. That spine is OK if you are reading a novel or an easy-to-absorb instructional volume. On the other hand, if you need to lay the book flat to follow a list of detailed instructions you need to place a heavy object on it so it stays open to a specific page. That heavy object can bend or break pages out of the spine and damaging the book probably is not what the reader wants to accomplish.

Spiral binding (outlined in Chapter 5-A: Printing at Home starting on page 53) is one solution. We think a coil-wire spine is the best allowing the book to lay flat while reviewing detailed instructions. So, how in the heck do you get a spiral binding on an already printed paperback book? There are two solutions—do it yourself or have Staples, Office Max, etc. do it for you.

If you decided to have an outside company like Staples do it for you, the cost will be between $8.00 and $10.00 (based on 2019 prices). They will cut off the spine and replace it with a spiral binding. We think that would be the best option if you are only doing a few personal books but if doing larger quantities to sell to customers you may want to consider doing the job in house and charging extra for the service.

We elected to do our spiral binding in-house and charge $5.00 for the service because we already have the needed equipment from our venture outlined in Chapter 5-A: Printing at Home (page 53). In addition to the binding punch we already had (Figure 5-41, cost about $100.00) we added a multi-page paper cutter (Figure 5-42, cost about $150.00) with the ability to cut several hundred pages at a time. With the pictured equipment we can cut the spine off of a POD paperback book and replace it with spiral binding.

Our equipment is not top of the line. If we were doing thousands of books rather than hundreds, we would definitely invest in higher-end equipment. For example, the hole punch in Figure 5-41 will only go through about 10 pages at a time. That means we have to apply the punch multiple times to prepare a book for binding and as a word of caution, it's really easy to misalign one group of 10 pages which can really mess up a book but there

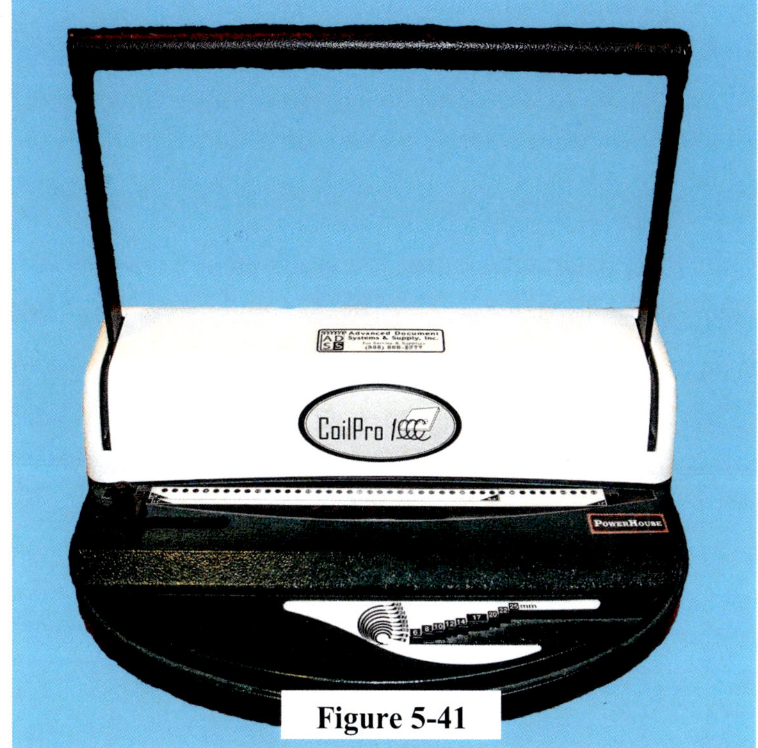

Figure 5-41

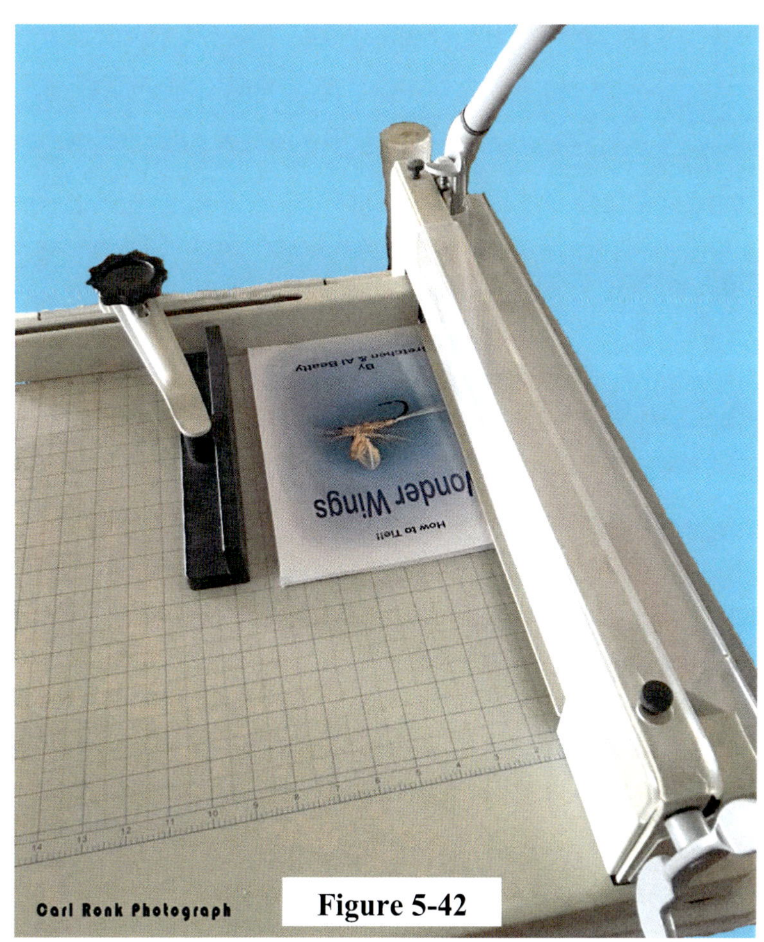

Figure 5-42

is a workaround. We can use the cutter in Figure 5-42 on the previous page to lightly trim the edges of the book if needed but we really prefer to do an accurate job in the first place. Before getting the cutter, Al often “evened up books” using his wood-shop belt sander; it did a fairly decent job and can be had at Harbor Freight for about $50.00.

While discussing the cutter, the inexpensive one we purchased claims to cut “up to 400 pages” at a time. We don’t think it would actually cut many 400-page books before something broke. We’ve cut books up to 200 pages (100 pieces of paper plus two paperback covers) effortlessly but really doubt it would handle more pages without eventual problems.

Figure 5-43

Illustrated in Figure 5-43 is the three stages of removing a spine and adding a spiral binding. The reason you see the red circle and square is to bring another option to your attention. Before purchasing the cutter, Al got the idea he could complete the job using his woodworking table saw. That option sort-of-worked but just barely. A regular carbide-tip-circular saw blade tends to tear up the cover’s corners and edges. See the book’s corner in the illustration above. If we had elected to buy an 80-tooth blade, the results may have been better but the actual paper cutter made for the job produces a neat, even edge (pictured center above) so that’s what we bought. You’ll have to make your purchase decision based on your needs.

Food for thought: If an instructor needs a small booklet for a class handout or something similar, then it’s easy to put TWO PAGES on top of each other so they print on the same piece of paper. Instructors will then have two documents after cutting the page in half each 5.5” by 8.5.”

What other options are possible? Make four mini booklets by cutting a paperback in half BOTH ways, cutting off any spines, and replace with spiral binding. Or, put together a 25-page book twice so you can divide it in the middle after cutting off the spine. Use the instructions on page 55 to manufacture covers then trim if needed.

Chapter 6—Audio & Video

OK readers, we are back at that imaginary stop sign discussed in Chapter 3: The Cross Roads on page 17. Being back at the same place again makes you wonder if we are just going in circles. Never fear, our next turn (to the right) takes us in the direction of this book's last pages. That said, we still have a couple of things to discuss, audio and video.

We also have a bit of a dilemma because we have a lot of video experience (starting in the late 80s) but we have NEVER produced an audiobook of any of our published work. So, why are we telling you about audiobook production when we've never had the experience and why have we never produced an audiobook? That's a good question. Read on for the answer.

All of our books are how-to-do-it, instructional-intensive volumes using many illustrations or photographs to support the informational text. We think an author who wants to share instructional information on any given topic needs illustrations to provide clarity to the lesson plan. It's doesn't make any difference whether that information is how to construct a fishing fly (like our work) or how to assemble-and-soldier a circuit board on a computer. We think a picture is worth a thousand words and this book has more than 125 of them.

Audiobooks are recordings of a "person" reading the text to save the listener from having to do so. It's a great option for a number of reasons including people with a disability; distraction for a person doing a repetitive task; or driving down the highway to an outdoor adventure like we often enjoy. We really like audiobooks by Tom Clancy, James Patterson, Clive Cussler, and Rob Dircks just to name a few. Hearing a person read them while traveling changes an otherwise boring trip into an adventure to a far-off place or to never-never-land.

On the other hand, the instructional books like those we publish are next to impossible to read because we've never figured out how to "read a picture" to another person. That's probably why we've never found an audiobook that explained in detail how to assemble a piece of electronic gear. Quite frankly, they (audiobooks) are much better for painting a mental picture of an imaginary adventure.

Ok, you already know we write books chocked full of fly-tying information and have no experience with audiobooks but this tome is an exploration on the topic of self-publishing. We thought it was a good idea to at least give you an idea what you'll be up against if producing an audiobook is a personal goal. Besides, we have a lot of audio experience as part of video production so we can easily decipher audio terminology for you. You already know by referencing this chapter's title that we'll soon be discussing video production.

For now, we'll turn to a self-published author who is also an audiobook expert having directed, produced, and narrated his own work, Rob Dircks. If the name sounds familiar return to the previous page where we discussed favorite audiobook authors we enjoy while traveling to our next on-the-water adventure.

If you are interested in learning more about Rob we offer (with his permission) the following information from his website:

> " Rob Dircks is the Audible bestselling author of *Where the Hell is Tesla? The Wrong Unit, Don't Touch the Blue Stuff!*, and *You're Going to Mars!* He also writes, narrates and produces original sci-fi short stories for his monthly podcast series titled *Listen To The Signal* (Listen To The Signal.com). Connect with him at RobDircks.com or on Twitter at @RobDircks."

He also has a thorough tutorial on his website about self-publishing your audiobook (https://robdircks.com/yes-you-can-record-your-own-audiobook-heres-how/). There you can learn how to get an online audiobook account (ACX), what recording equipment you will need, how to set up a studio, what recording parameters you must follow, assembling and editing your audio clips, and the list goes on. Also, we recommend joining us as subscribers to his YouTube channel. You can access it at the top of the webpage tutorial listed above. It contains a wealth of self-publishing information.

Those topics are important. You can check how Rob's gear works by going to his podcast website and listening to the audio quality he can produce with his equipment. On the other hand, if you want to give-it-a-try without investing roughly $500 in recording gear (assuming you already have a computer) we'll offer equipment options you probably already have available.

Our recording studio is so simple it will probably make all of you chuckle. Even though it's a bit "makeshift," it gets the job done with a little "adjusting" on our part. What do we use? It's our Android IOS Smartphone but for those of you who have an iPhone, it will work equally well. A tablet of one type or another is also a good option but we don't have one yet. For the rest of this discussion we'll just refer to our device as a "phone" and let you fill in the brand, model, etc. specifications.

To get good sound from our phone we need a place to do our recording that has no background noise. Things we live with every day (fans, air conditioner, vehicle traffic, conversation, etc.) will play havoc with your sound recording.

We tried a number of places in and around our home. One of the two best was in the front seat of our car parked inside the garage with blankets draped from each window. The other was standing in Al's clothes closet with enough clothing pushed aside to provide him a space to read the text standing up. The important item with each location was the "fabric" that surrounded it. The fabric acted as a damper stopping most of the bounced sound that causes an echo in any audio recording. Both sites produced great audio at the expense of the reader's (Al) comfort. The garage/car was either too hot or cold and standing in the closet reading a book into a recorder was even less fun than the car-in-the-garage idea!

Gretchen offered the best solution when she suggested we use a blanket to enclose a corner of our cedar-paneled, basement rec-room. The 3- x 4-foot enclosure (Figure 6-1) provided just enough room for a light, rolling office chair, and a tripod with a clamp to hold the phone steady. In fact, it was the same device we already used to shoot video with the phone. Bottom line, the studio cost nothing and actually worked. In time though, the walls did close in making a coffee break most welcome!

Figure 6-1

After some experimenting, we discovered placing a POP filter between the reader and the phone's microphone produced the best sound quality. A POP filter is a piece of cloth on a clamp arm that easily mounts on a stand or tripod. It's designed to reduce the "annoying sound" when pronouncing "p, f, or th." They're on eBay for $15.00.

There are a number of free phone recording app's available and two we tried were RecForge II and Smart Recorder. We thought Smart Recorder (illustrated in Figure 6-1) was easier to use and settled on it. Once the WAV files were transferred to our computer via a USB cable, the need for audio-editing software was the next thing on our "needs list."

We downloaded the free version of WavPad (https://www.nch.com.au/wavepad/) and found it did a good job on the tests we ran with it. That said, we already had

Adobe's Photoshop Elements 15 (PSE) and Premiere Elements 15 (PRE) that we use when teaching video-photography classes. PRE is also the video editing software we use for the films on our YouTube channel. It didn't take us long to figure out the video editing program (PRE) was also an audio editor and we already knew its commands. Familiarity made it easier to use than any of the free programs we tried. Also, it doesn't cost much considering its versatility. We did a quick eBay search and found a used, older version for about $10.00 and a new version for about $75.00. If a person wanted a combo package of both programs (PSE and PRE), the new version runs about $100.00 but if you watch the sales at Costco you can get both for about $70.00.

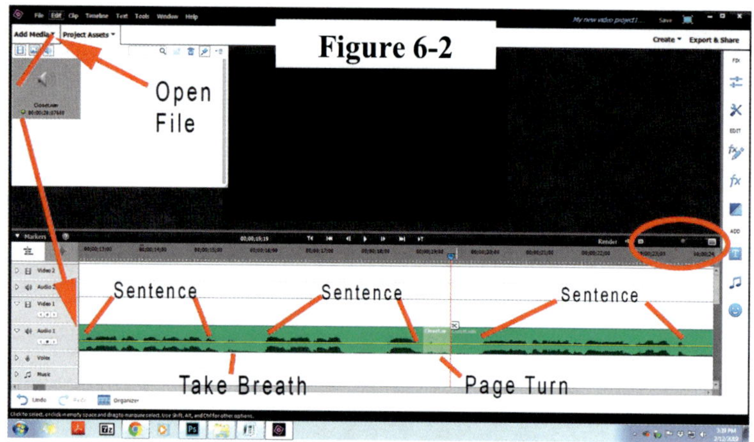

Figure 6-2

Editing audio on the PRE video editor is just as easy as it is to edit video. Figure 6-2 illustrates PRE 15 with the test audio file captured in Al's closet. Notice where the files are imported (red arrow with "Open File"), then follow the lines with the red arrow ending at the "Audio 1" timeline. We've identified the three sentences with a break between each. There is a small amount of noise when Al took a breath between the first two sentences that we elected to leave as is. However, the noise made by turning the page is distracting so we'll remove it by dragging the position bar (fine red line) to the start of the noise and click on the scissor icon. Then we move the position bar to the end of the noise and again click on the scissor icon. Clicking directly on the timeline BETWEEN the two scissor cuts will highlight that section. When we press the delete key on our computer that page-turn noise disappears and we can go to the next position on the timeline we'd like to edit. NOTE: There is a light-colored dot in the center of the red circle. We slide that dot back and forth to adjust the amount of space the audio file displays on the timeline.

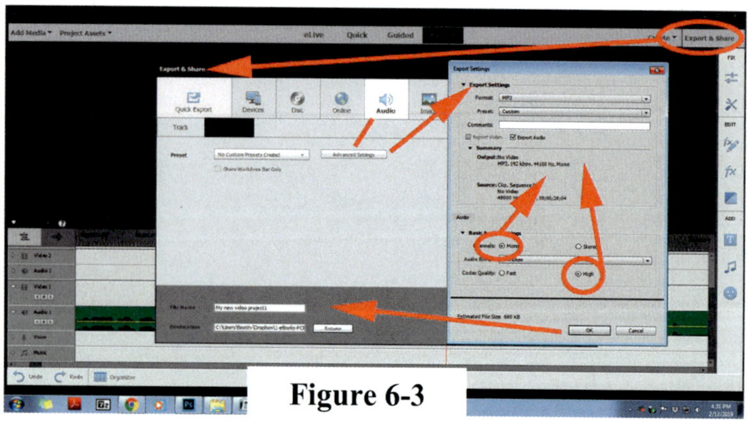
Figure 6-3

Once the audio editing is complete we need to save our work in the proper format for an audiobook. Start in the upper right corner of Figure 6-3 and click "Export & Share" to open the options menu you see here. Follow the arrows to access the "Custom" settings. Notice the two red circles toward the bottom of the options menu. Be sure to select **Mono** for the audio and **High** for quality. Those two selections automatically adjust the audio to these important settings—MP3, 192 kbps, 44100Hz, Mono. MP3 = the file type; 192 kbps = 192 kilobits per second transfer speed; 44100 Hz = 44.1 thousand Hertz frequency; and Mono = the channel output type. After clicking OK, the red arrow takes us to the place where we identify the file's name and location on our computer.

Now that you have seen how to process a file, you'll need to read the chapters into your recorder making certain each is in its own separate file. Then edit each chapter to take out gaps, noises, and other unwanted "stuff" to prepare your book for publishing on Amazon's Audible website (https://www.acx.com/).

So, if reading, recording, and producing your own book sounds like more darned trouble than you want, there are other options available through the ACX website. Figure 6 -4 is a screen capture of the ACX home page. Along the top of the page are drop-down menu options. We've highlighted the "How It Works" menu with red arrows pointed at two selections. They are "Author" and "Narrator" options though you can readily see others as well. When you click the "Author" tab the screen illustrated in Figure 6-5 is loaded. We've expanded the section "Audio Production Resources" to bring it to your attention. That section contains a wealth of information of which you should have a basic understanding before attempting to hire help with your audiobook.

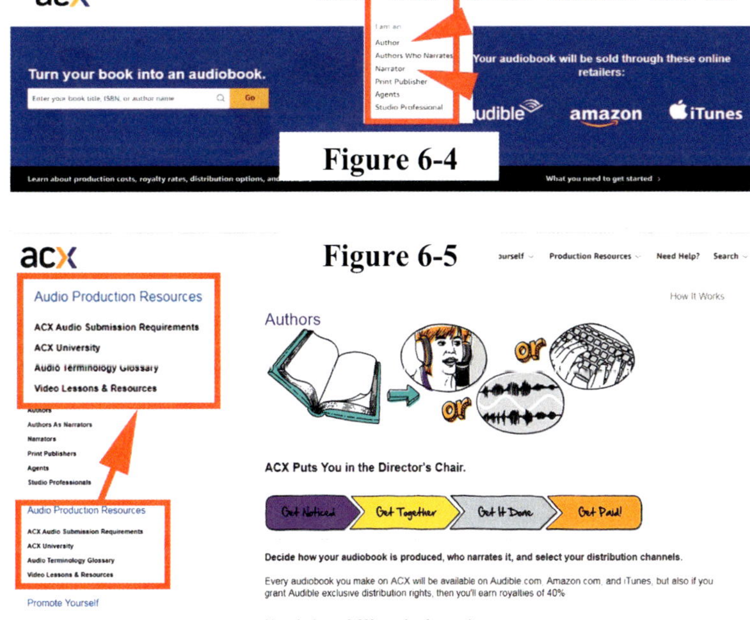

Figure 6-4

Figure 6-5

The "Search" tab produces two options; "Producers For Hire" and "Titles Accepting Auditions." If you want someone to do the work there are options. First, you can hire a producer to do it all or you can hire an actor/narrator to convert your book into an audio file that you produce yourself. There are a number of methods for paying the producers and actors which include payment-in-dollars or in some cases the person will do the work in exchange for part of the royalties. If you are an unknown author, you'll probably find your professional help will be more interested in getting paid dollars rather than getting a "piece of the action." In case you are interested as of February 2019 the ACX site had 1,426 titles open for audition, 80, 262 producers looking for work, and 140,280 audiobooks for sale. Given that today (2019) audiobooks only account for about 5% of the market there is a lot of room for growth.

Where the audiobook market will go for here we are not sure but we are definitely excited about the potential that future years will bring. As discussed earlier in this chapter, we've not found audiobooks a good fit for the type of illustration intensive books we write.

We do use the audiobook concept to produce short 5-minute introductory audio MP3 files to post on our website aimed at helping a potential customer decide to purchase a book. The audio files work well in that situation because we can pick and choose information for the audio file that doesn't require pictures to share the idea.

We understand we are leaving you "dangling" in reference to audiobooks. Sorry, but as stated earlier we've just not found a use for them. If you decide to venture into audiobooks we'll leave you with two thoughts. When you lay out your cover it MUST be in a square format and (this is IMPORTANT) you **can not publish** an audiobook on ACX (Amazon) unless it is **already published** with them as a paperback or eBook.

Regarding the square cover: Do not think you can just put a colored box around an already-published book's rectangular cover. ACX will not accept your "reworked" cover. You'll have to lay it out in a square format specifically for your audiobook.

The last item before leaving this section on audiobooks: We've found the free version of VLC media player (https://www.videolan.org/vlc/) to play just about any type of **video** or **audio** file. It is much easier to use than opening your Premiere Elements (PRE) editing program to listen to an audio file.

Video: The VLC program is a great way to switch from the audio part of this chapter to the video. For us, it's a transition from a publishing discipline with minimal personal experience (audio) to one with a much wider knowledge base (video with audio).

Al got his introduction to video production in the late 80s while producing technical training films for the telephone industry. For him, the transition from training films for corporate America to those focused on fly fishing and fly tying was as natural as water off a duck's back. By the time we were married in the early 90s, he was already proficient in the technical side of video production. Gretchen brought strong classroom skill set to Team Beatty adding an important spark to our video production(s). When we retired from corporate life soon after our wedding, it became an important part of our fledgling outdoor-focused business. BT's Fly Fishing Products was the new company's name. We were confident there could be a life after corporate American and set out to prove it—with tenacity and determination.

As the next years unfolded, video production remained an important part of our day-to-day business until the exploding popularity of the free-for-everyone YouTube phenomenon brought it to a screeching halt. It didn't take us long though to figure out giving away something (video) wasn't all bad as long we didn't give it ALL away. What do we mean by that statement? We learned to "repurpose" our videos by using them as marketing tools rather than as profit centers. In the process, we carefully dipped our toes into the new **Internet** marketing world. It was quite a step into the "unknown" for us but we soon learned that YouTube is great for marketing while also providing instruction for those looking for help.

That's the purpose of this section; to offer guidance in producing your own YouTube and other online videos to use as you see fit. For us, you already know we use them to market our books by giving the reader a free " taste" of what can be found in other chapters after making a purchase. If the viewer goes no further than watching the YouTube clip, they still walk away with gained knowledge. On the other hand, if that same reader decides the free "taste" of the book's content is not enough and they decide to purchase it; viewer and author both have gained something.

In this section, we'll share with you our "shoe-string" approach to online video. In short order, you'll soon see our video-production methods are very similar to our barebones approach to audio production. Let's start with our simple equipment setup.

We'll break that equipment down into three basic categories—lighting, cameras, and audio. All are equally important and of the three you'll probably be surprised to learn that quality audio is the most important **video** item and is also the more difficult to achieve. Therefore, we'll leave it until last.

Lighting: We think THIS is the second most important aspect of any video including those distributed through YouTube (YT) or other online outlets. Without good light, it is really difficult to see what the presenter is offering. Unfortunately, all too often an aspiring YT videographer will simply turn on his/her "phone" (remember we simply call ALL cell phones, iPhones, and Smartphones just phones!), hold it at arm's length, and start talking. The resulting YT video might be OK but usually swings more toward terrible than it does toward good. All this aspiring YT videographer would have to do to improve a terrible video to an OK one would be to add a few inexpensive lights.

We know the word "few" is somewhat ambiguous so let's take a look at the lighting arrangement we use to capture our fly-tying instructional YT videos. In Figure 6-6, you can readily see we have 5 lights in our basic setup. Off camera, we also have a 4-head, ceiling-mounted track lighting system over our fly-tying work area to supplement the room's double-bulb light fixture. Of the 5 lights in our basic setup, 4 of them are simple swing-arm lamps (red circles) used only for video and are available at Staples, Office Max, etc. for about $15.00 each. The 5th lamp (red arrow) is Al's regular work light. Gretchen also has a similar unit above her workspace.

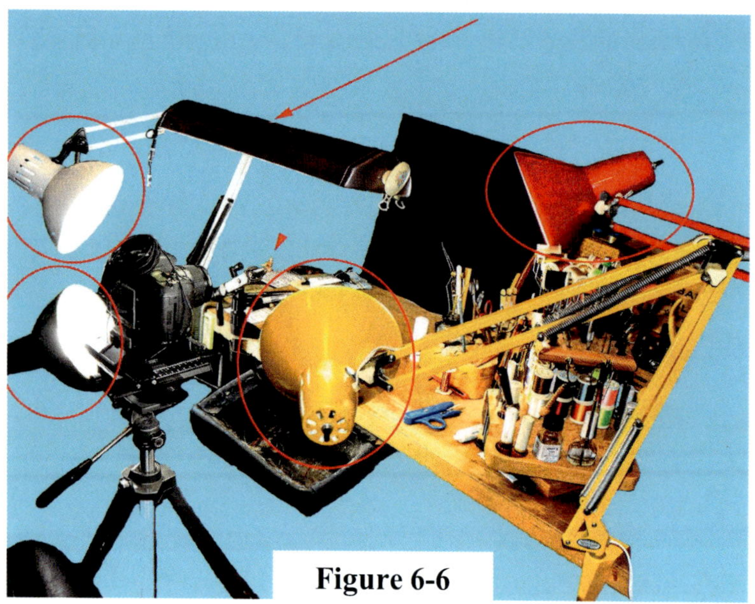

Figure 6-6

We use day-light balanced, 100-watt equivalent low energy LED light bulbs in the 4-video lights because they last a long time and provide clean-video illumination. We are using 500 watts of light that produces a well-lit video of the subject (a fishing fly). Before we leave this paragraph on the quantity of illumination, note that 3 of the lights are in **front** of the subject-fly (mini-red arrowhead), 1 is **slightly behind** it (provides separation from the black background), and Al's work light is **directly above.**

The other part of the film is Al making the introduction (Figure 6-7). During his on-camera time, we reposition two of the lamps so one is pointed at his face and the other is slightly behind to provide separation from the background. The ceiling mounted track lighting provides fill light to reduce the shadows on his face. Note Al is using his phone to film the introduction. We'll discuss that in a few minutes.

Figure 6-7

Cameras: If you again check the illustrations on the previous page, you can readily see we are using two cameras, a Nikon DSLR and a phone. Yes, we hate to admit after spending many dollars, that one of our go-to cameras is a phone. The darned thing takes great pictures and video. The audio is also good if we use a lavaliere microphone or our shoe-string studio to reduce ambient noise, distortion, etc. but we'll discuss audio more in a few minutes.

You have probably guessed by now about 95% of our video productions are recorded in our fly-tying workroom. Almost all of the resulting video is instructional how-to-do-it footage on assembling different fly-fishing components (lures & flies). That means we spend very little time in-the-field capturing video footage. When we do go afield the phone is our video camera of choice. Figure 6-8 illustrates how we set it up to easily capture field footage. In the picture are the phone, a phone clip, an L-bracket handle, a 9-volt battery powered radio frequency microphone receiver, and two 9-volt battery powered lavaliere microphones. The thing we want to focus on here is the L-bracket and the clip to hold the phonc. Λlso, no tice the 'pod attachment on the bottom of the L-bracket. We use that on the rare occasion when a tripod or monopod becomes a necessity; it doesn't happen often but it's there if we need it.

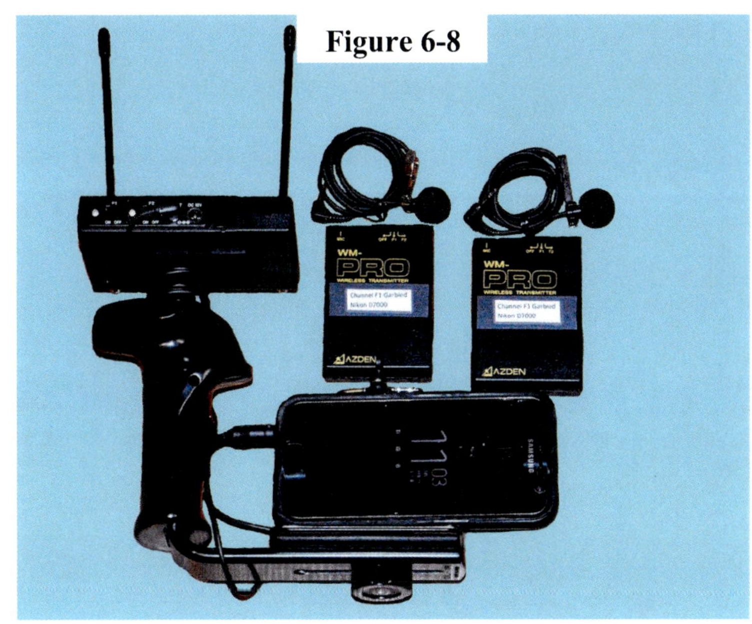

Figure 6-8

The reason we use the tripod-mounted phone (Figure 6-7 on the previous page) is the focus. You already know we are quite pleased with the video/audio the phone will capture but the "almost instantaneous focus" is impressive. If we use our DSLR cameras, the automatic focus is slow at best. Yes, a lot of movie and TV studios use DSLRs for their work but they also have a person whose job is "pulling focus." We don't have that luxury so we use the auto setting on the front-facing camera so Al can verify he is in the frame. He can move around (as long as he remains in-the-frame) and the focus changes so fast it's almost impossible to see it. Also, the auto exposure changes just as fast. If we need to switch the phone to all-manual shooting, we just make that selection from its menu (swipe left-to-right across the screen to access it) then select the shooting options individually based on our needs at that particular time.

Before we move on from shooting with a phone let's talk about several more things that will help you capture better video footage. These may seem too simple to even discuss but the reason we are doing so is we've made these same mistakes.

First, when filming with your phone, place it in airplane mode (or do-not-disturb mode) so an incoming call or text doesn't mess up that perfect video clip. Next, clean the lens before starting a shoot to be sure any stray dust, dirt, or fingerprints are eliminated! When videoing yourself (or another person) look straight at the camera. Connect with your audience by looking them in the eye. Last, shoot in an environment that matches the film's content. In other words, don't shoot a fly-tying video in a woodworking shop. Don't think these tips only apply when shooting with a phone, they are also important when using a higher end camera. Now is as good of a time as any to take a look at using a high-end DSLR.

Figure 6-9

Figure 6-10

A DSLR camera is our choice for the stationary focus, in-one-spot instructions, that encompass about 80% of our videos—how-to-construct fly-fishing paraphernalia. The lighting arrangement we use is detailed on page 92 (Figure 6-6) if you'd like to refresh your memory. Figure 6-9 illustrates how we set up our DSLR to capture macro video. Mounted on the camera is a 30-year old manual-focus, macro lens. Plugged into the camera is a Boya By-M1 Lavaliere Microphone illustrated in Figure 6-10. Notice it has a switch on its battery compartment. When it's pushed to the up position, the mic is ready for use on a camera. If it in the down position, it is ready to use on a phone.

The "B-Lav," as we call it, requires a small battery (SR44 or equivalent) when used on a DSLR but it functions just fine on a phone with no battery **or** the power switch in the OFF position. What's great about this microphone is it cost about $20.00 online.

For years we struggled with "changing light" in our videos caused by our hands moving through the video frame and blocking some of the light. That would cause the subject in the video to get dark when our hands enter the frame to perform an on-camera function. When we'd take our hand out of the shot, the picture's lighting would return to normal.

We tried EVERYTHING to find a solution and finally discovered what we'll share next. If you've had a similar problem, you may find our camera "settings" useful. They are select "M" for manual; set the shutter speed to 1/60; turn the lens aperture ring to f-16 *; set the white balance to AWB (automatic); select average light metering; and set the ISO to automatic. The automatic ISO was THE answer. It changes so fast you don't even know it's compensating for the changing light in your video frame.

- = Every lens/camera combination has a "sweet spot" where the two units together produce the sharpest image they can. On our Nikon D7000 + the all-manual macro lens, it's f-16. Our other camera/lens combination varies from one to the next. The best way to find your camera's sweet spot is to shoot a series of fixed-focus pictures starting at f-8 then advancing up to as high as the lens will go (ours is f-16). Check the pictures and one of them will stand out as sharper than the rest. That f-stop setting is the sweet spot for the two-unit combination.

Whether to shoot high-resolution video or not is up to you. A camera shooting video in high-definition (1080p) uses a little over 2 million bites (MB) of storage space per SECOND of shooting time and that's not the highest definition many of today's cameras will capture. Almost all newer cameras will capture 4K video and that eats up about 6.25 MB per SECOND of shooting time; it will completely fill a 16 GB (gigabit) card in 40 minutes. That's a huge storage requirement.

We understand we advised shooting as high of a resolution as possible for our still pictures but high-definition video uses storage to the point of ridiculous. When the video is destined for a YouTube (YT) posting, the uploading process will automatically reduce the video file size so we make our captures using one of the lower resolution settings. If we do a good job of lighting the scene, it will look good on YT.

Audio, in our opinion, is one of the most important components of a quality video. What's amazing is it is also the easiest to talk about. It's like copy editing text that we reviewed in Chapters 4-D and 5-G; if its right there's not much else to do. If it's wrong it needs to be fixed and audio is no different. If the audio is good, you won't even notice it but if is not what you are watching will scream "bad, bad, bad" VERY loud and clear.

So what do we (and you) do to get good audio? We've already covered it to some extent in our discussion about audiobooks. You must either use a sound studio (real or makeshift) or use noise mitigating audio equipment. The best option is to use both but in the real world that is not always possible. Take our audiobook recording mini-studio illustrated in Figure 6-1 on Page 87. It has polar fleece blankets on all sides and a carpet on the flour. The sound is quite good given we are recording with a simple phone with NO extra audio equipment. Take a close look at Figure 6-1 and notice how the corners of the picture are also dark. That's because in that simple, shoe-string studio both audio AND light will not bounce. There the camera flash we used to capture the picture only went where it was aimed; there was no bounce whatsoever. Sound works the same way but you just can't see it. You sure as heck will hear it though if you have smooth walls; it will show up in the form of distortion and echo.

The lavaliere microphone illustrated in Figure 6-10 on page 94 is another way of reducing echo in your video's audio soundtrack. Notice we said "reduce echo," we didn't mention eliminating it. We'll talk more about "cleaning up audio" starting in the next paragraph about video editing.

Video editing is a subject that can be as easy or complex as you wish to make it. We have friends who edit ALL of their videos on their phone and do a really good job at it. On the other end of the pendulum, we have a couple of friends who shoot video footage for National Geographic and their editing "suite" is beyond our comprehension. It includes thousands of dollars in hard drives, processors, and multiple monitors. Compared to us, they are very high end. We tend to operate a slightly above the editing-on-a-phone crowd but way below the high-end people. Like our shoe-string audio studio, our video editing suite is an old Window 7 PC with a single monitor. You've already seen the program we use earlier in this chapter, Adobe Premiere Elements (PRE) version 15.

PRE is a very functional, inexpensive editing software we use for our YT videos and our sound recordings. It works on the timeline concept like many other editing programs. If you don't know what a timeline is playing any YT video. You'll see the video start to run and the "progress arrow" advances from the left side of the control track. It's finished when it reaches the right side. The picture and audio change as the arrow moves from left to right. That left-right movement represents time and it moves along the line under the picture; thus the name "timeline." Another way to look at it, a video/audio timeline is the digital equivalent of a strip of movie file. It is a series of pictures with accompanying audio. Those pictures are normally captured at a rate of 30 frames per second (fps) however that can vary depending on the video type and style (EX: slow motion, frame-rate standards like NTSC, PAL, or SECAM). For this discussion, we'll assume the video is 30 fps. We hope this quick explanation is not too basic.

Figure 6-11 below illustrates a PRE timeline from a recent video we uploaded to You-Tube (YT). In the picture we've identified several component with red text. We've included definitions for each below the picture.

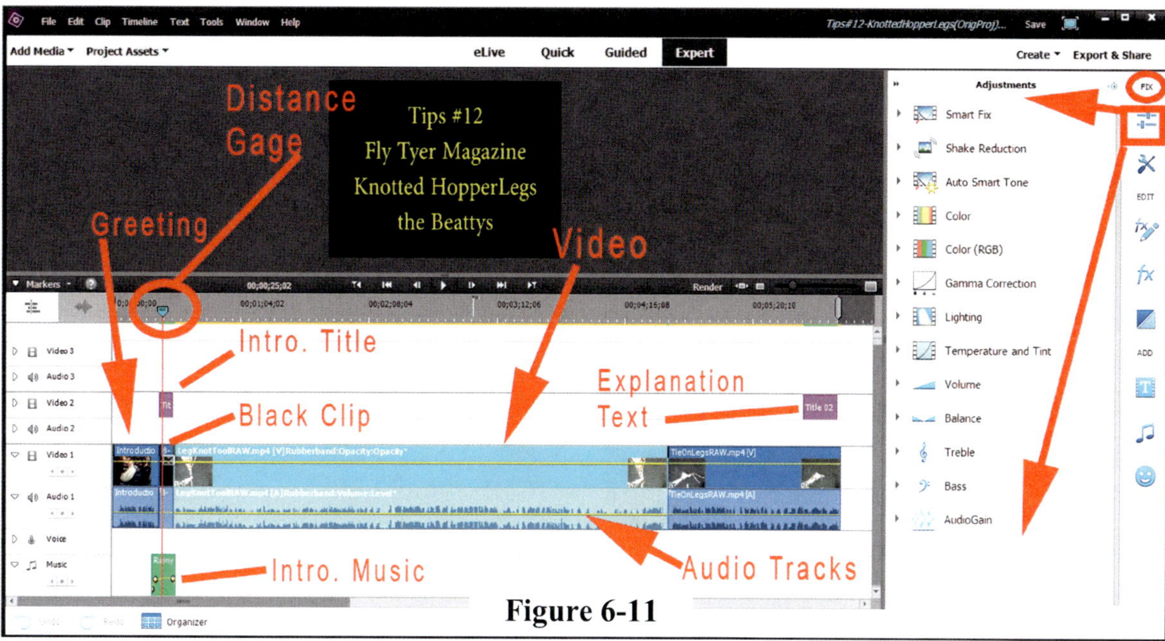

Figure 6-11

Let's start with the two parts of the timeline itself—**Video** and **Audio Tracks**. On the far left-hand side of the picture, you'll see two identifiers—Video 1 and Audio 1. If you look carefully, you will see the timeline is comprised of 4-video clips and we have the third one from the left activated. You can tell it's activated by that section's brighter color. The **Video** part of the track is the 30-picture-frames-per-second unit and below it are two **Audio Tracks—**left and right.

We mention the **Audio Track** because when we first recorded these video/audio clips we were using an old single-track microphone and only one of those "squiggly audio lines" was present. We wanted a person listening to our YT video to hear audio on both sides of the headphones or speakers. We felt it needed to be fixed.

To change that we went to the **FIX** menu selection (red circle at upper right). There are several hundred menu options so we're not going to illustrate them all but if you search through them you'll find an audio correction section. The option we used to change the audio from single-track mono to stereo is called Fill Right From Left. That correction produces stereo audio from a single track by copying the sound in the left track to the right track. As already stated there are hundreds of options there to fix or edit both audio and video. If you elect to use PRE as we have, be sure to do yourself a favor and spend some time perusing through those options. The things this simple program can do are mind-boggling, at least to us anyway!

On the previous page, we got sidetracked so let's get back to talking about the components of the timeline in addition to the video and audio tracks. Let's start with the **Greeting**. We commence most of our YT videos with a short greeting in which one of us (usually Al) starts by telling the audience hello, who we are, and what we'll be discussing in the next few minutes.

After the initial greeting, we go to the **Intro. Title, Black Clip**, and **Intro. Music**. This section is usually about 10 seconds long so we start by "inserting" a 10-second clip of black video onto which we'll place a 10-second title. Then we add a short section of music to fill the dead-audio space in that clip. NOTE: We manufacture black video clips for this purpose using our DSLR and recording them using a stopwatch. We have a number of clips recorded starting at 2 seconds and going to 20 seconds. When recording them we make sure to turn off the camera's microphone so the clip is black video only with no sound.

The next item we'll talk about is what we call the **Distance Gage**. It is the little turquoise triangle on top of the thin red line. It indicates what you can see in the "viewing screen" that is displayed above the timeline. You can see we made this screen capture when it was positioned inside the video's title section. When that gage gets to the next video clip (the one that's activated) we'll be able to see the actual YT video content, more on that below.

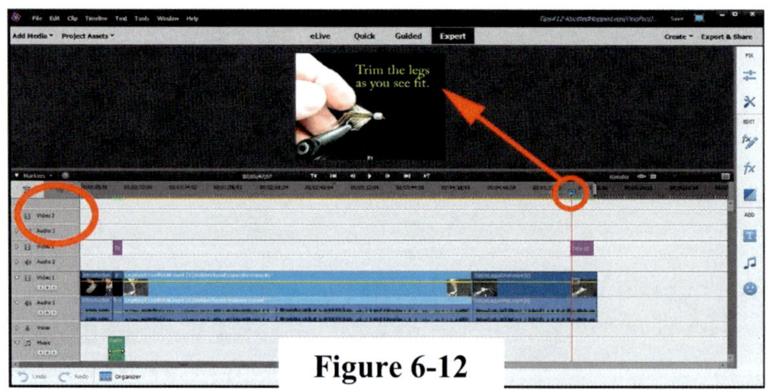

Figure 6-12

As you can see in Figure 6-12, the **Distance Gage** has advanced along the timeline almost to the end. We wanted to point out it has reached what we call **Explanation Text** that displays as part of the video picture. We use it to add further explanation where needed. Also note the black background we use for many of our YT videos. The black background provides good separation between the subject and the background. It's also a place for explanatory text when needed.

You are probably wondering why we have a red circle around the Video 3 and Audio 3 (AV) headings on the left side of the illustration. They identify a part of the timeline we've not discussed (or used) but we offer a little tip on how we often use it. The way a timeline works is the TOP AV will play OVER any below it. In other words, if we place a video clip (with audio removed) ABOVE the standard timeline the new video will be displayed while the original audio continues to play. This is called an "insert edit." We use this feature to "cut away" from the original video when needed. You see insert editing on TV all the time and may not know what was really happening. Here's an example: A TV anchor person is interviewing a down-hill skier while standing at the bottom of a snow-covered hill. During the course of the interview, the picture cuts away from the two people standing at the bottom of the ski slope and shows the skier zooming down the hill while you can still hear the two people progressing through the interview. After a few seconds of "cutaway video" it then returns to the two people and the interview continues. That "cutaway video" was an insert edit.

So, how do you use this for your YT videos? We could tell you we use the technique to provide better instructional content but in truth, we usually use it to cover up some kind of mistake. For example, while filming a recent video our dog Carley poked her nose into the frame when she sniffed the fly Al was filming in the vise. Imagine the picture displayed in Figure 6-12 if a dog's black nose suddenly appeared in the shot. We could start the capture over OR we just execute an insert edit of Al's hands picking up an item pertinent to the instruction in the video. That quick insert edit easily covered up the dog's nose without having to reshoot the whole segment. We know that would never happen to any of you but offer this option just in case it ever does!

Saving and uploading is the final part of our video. We ALWAYS SAVE the completed video as a file on our computer's hard drive (Figure 6-13, Export & Share) BEFORE uploading it to YouTube. Why? We don't want to lose our work. It's called back up!

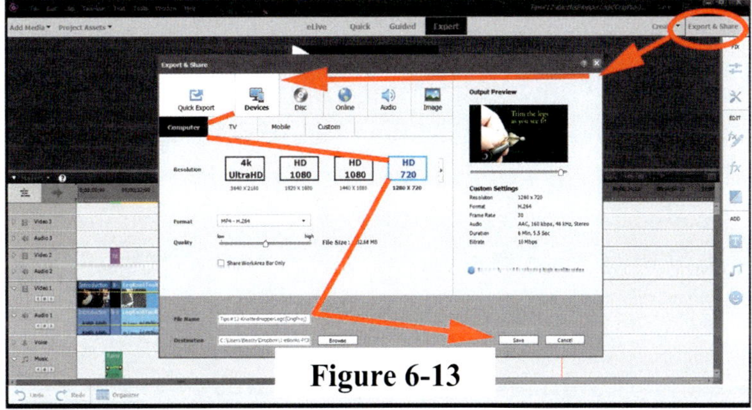

Figure 6-13

The UPLOADING process is similar to saving the file to your computer's hard drive. If you don't already have one, you must set up a YouTube account. After that follow the red arrows from Export & Share to your final destination. On our Internet connection, it takes about 8 minutes to upload 1 minute of content to YouTube. You'll have to see

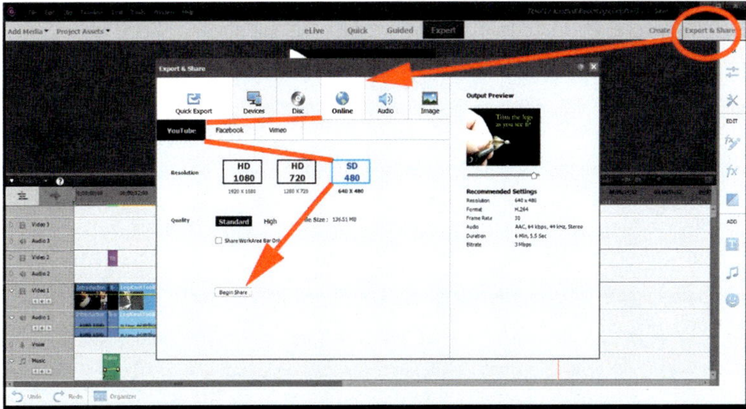

how long it takes using your Internet connection. Notice you also have other options via the Export & Share icon. They are Facebook and Vimeo should you be interested in placing your videos on those locations.

YouTube is an interesting phenomenon. We've heard that some people make a good living posting "stuff" on YT but we sure have not figured out how to get any more from it than enjoying a free place to share our videos with an audience.

The way we use our YT channel is to make a video of a chapter from one of our books then post it with the idea people will find it interesting then purchase the book from Amazon to receive additional information. Does it work? It seems to because our books create a fairly steady revenue stream. The dollars show up in our bank account each month. It's almost like Christmas when that happens.

We're not getting rich from self -publishing but we're doing as good or better than we did when working with a brick and mortar publishing house. We're not trying to denigrate ANY publishing house's reputation. They have a large expense they must recover to stay in business. They do ALL of the setup and pre-publishing work then upfront the cost of printing thousands of copies of a book that are expensive to keep in inventory until a customer decides to purchase a copy.

When you self-publish through Amazon's Kindle Direct Publishing (KDP) YOU do all of the setup and pre-publishing work. If your self-published tome is destined to be an eBook then it is simply a file sitting on a KDP server waiting for a customer to pay-to-download it. If you are selling print books through KDP your work is still just a file on one of their servers until an order for a book tells one of KDP's machines to print and send a paperback. Last if you are selling an audiobook again it is simply a file sitting on an ACX server waiting for a customer to pay-to-download it. The process is fairly straight forward and, to date, has treated us well.

Chapter 7—Closing comments

Quite frankly, we are in a bit of a quandary. Why! Because this book is supposed to be an encyclopedia on self-publishing and we have only scratched the surface of what we think the idea can offer. In our opinion, the do-it-yourself (DIY) concept is changing the publishing industry similar to what digital technology did to the photography industry about 20 years ago.

What do we think is on the horizon and spanning on into the future? It's only logical that in a few years every home will have a 3-dimensional printer that can produce in the home what has to be purchased and shipped today. The same goes for the Print On Demand (POD) idea for books. It's only a matter of time before our office printers can also print and bind our books. This idea may seem far fetched but think about it. It was only a few years ago we were using dot-matrix printers in our home and business offices. Today those same "printers" can turn out museum-quality photographs, scan text or pictures, function as a copy machine, and the list goes on!

In reflecting on this book's ending, we also took a look back at our lives and those of our parents. Our parents lived through the time in this world where technology went from the horse and buggy to the moon. In our lives, Al well remembers his early years on a dairy farm in northwest Iowa where a tractor AND a team of horses were both used on a regular basis. Years ago we both read Dick Tracy comic books where Mr. Tracy communicated through his watch; it was a real science-fiction concept at that point in history. Today ALL of the things Dick Tracy's watch could do are a reality AND a whole lot more! What comes next? We are not sure but for now, let's get back to today's real world.

Our purpose with this book was to share with you what we've learned about digital photography, the self-publishing business, and how YOU can put them together to become a published author. Almost everyone in this world is an expert on one subject or another.

You may think you have nothing to offer in the way of being an author and that could, in fact, be true but we really doubt it. We would love to find an instructional book that teaches an older couple like us how to really use our Smartphone (or iPhone) to its full potential. We use that wonderfully yet frustrating tool for a lot of things but when we watch our grandkids jump around their phones we find out how little we really know about them.

Phones aren't the only subject you might be an expert on. We like to do DIY projects around the house and being able to use a welder, or a volt-ohm meter, or build a cedar hot tub, or ....???? You get the idea? We hope so and that's why we think everyone is an expert at something. One of our joys in life is learning new things and it's people like you who teach us how to do our next DIY project.

Now we're Passing The Mantle" to all of you. Become a published author by writing about something you know and then branch out from there. We've been long recognized as knowledgeable (maybe expert) fly-fishing authors. Today, we are writing a book teaching YOU how to self publish. How much do you think we knew that topic three years ago? Zero! Zip! Natta! We are here to tell you that even an old dog (person) can learn new tricks

We know where we are pointing YOU with this book but where do WE go from here? We're not sure but we've set a personal goal to research and learn more about online marketing and how it can help us better share our books. Maybe our next non-fly-fishing book will be about online marketing or ... who knows! You can be sure of one thing, we have no intention of sitting down and "vegging" in front of the television. No, we'll be working on one project or another AND watching for YOUR new book. Good luck with your venture into the self-publishing world. We hope your journey will be as much fun as ours. Until then, take care & ...

Tight Lines—Gretchen & Al Beatty
Boise, Idaho
Spring 2019

Final thought: We saw this Amazon Prime delivery van just down the street from us. It's the one who delivers each new shipment of our books. Could it be making a book delivery to you! You'll never know until you give it a try. The ball's in your court! NOW, GO FOR IT!

About The Authors

Gretchen & Al Beatty are long time fly fishers, fly tiers, photographers, and writers from Boise, Idaho. They are best friends at the vise, on the water, at the computer keyboard, and behind the camera. When they are not working, they enjoy spoiling their four grandchildren. If you are interested, you can review their many DVDs and books on their website (www.btsflyfishing.com) or communicate with them using e-mail (albeatty2@aol.com).

The Beatty's books are also available via a download or paperback purchase at Amazon (www.amazon.com, type "Gretchen Al Beatty books" in the search engine). They offer subjects ranging from fly fishing, to candy making, and to self-publishing. Try them, you'll be glad you did!

Read, learn and enjoy!

GAB Publishing
A Division of
BT's Fly Fishing & Photography
Boise, Idaho

Made in the USA
Columbia, SC
18 February 2022

56400667R00060